CW01171433

theQueenstownbook

Jenny McLeod

The Queenstown Book

(Fourth Edition Reprint)
www.thequeenstownbook.co.nz

Published by Compact Productions Queenstown New Zealand

Copyright© Compact Productions 2011

First Published 1988, Second Edition 1990, Third Edition 1996,
Third Edition Reprints 1999, 2002
Fourth Edition 2007

ISBN-978-0-473-12646-9

Photographs by Rich Bayley www.richbayleyphotography.co.nz
(pages 2-3, 4-5, 8-9, 12 -13, 14, 16-17, 18, 22-23,
32-33, 34, 37, 46, 48-49, 57, 59, 74-75)

Euan Sarginson (pages 15, 19)

Text by Jenny McLeod

Designed by Feast Creative www.feast.co.nz

Printed by APOL Incorporating Phoenix Offset & Bookbuilders
Suite 1, 4 West Street, Pymble, NSW 2073, Australia. Printed in China.

All rights reserved. No part of this publication may be reproduced
or transmitted in any form or by any means, electronic or mechanical,
including photocopying, recording, storage in any information retrieval
system or otherwise, without the written permission of the publisher.

contents

Map	6
Introduction	7
Queenstown	9
Early Queenstown	20
Lake Wakatipu	24
The Shotover Valley	36
Wakatipu Countryside	44
Arrowtown	52
Gibbston	58
Mountains	62
Glenorchy	72

Left: St Joseph's Church   Following page: Queenstown from Bob's Peak

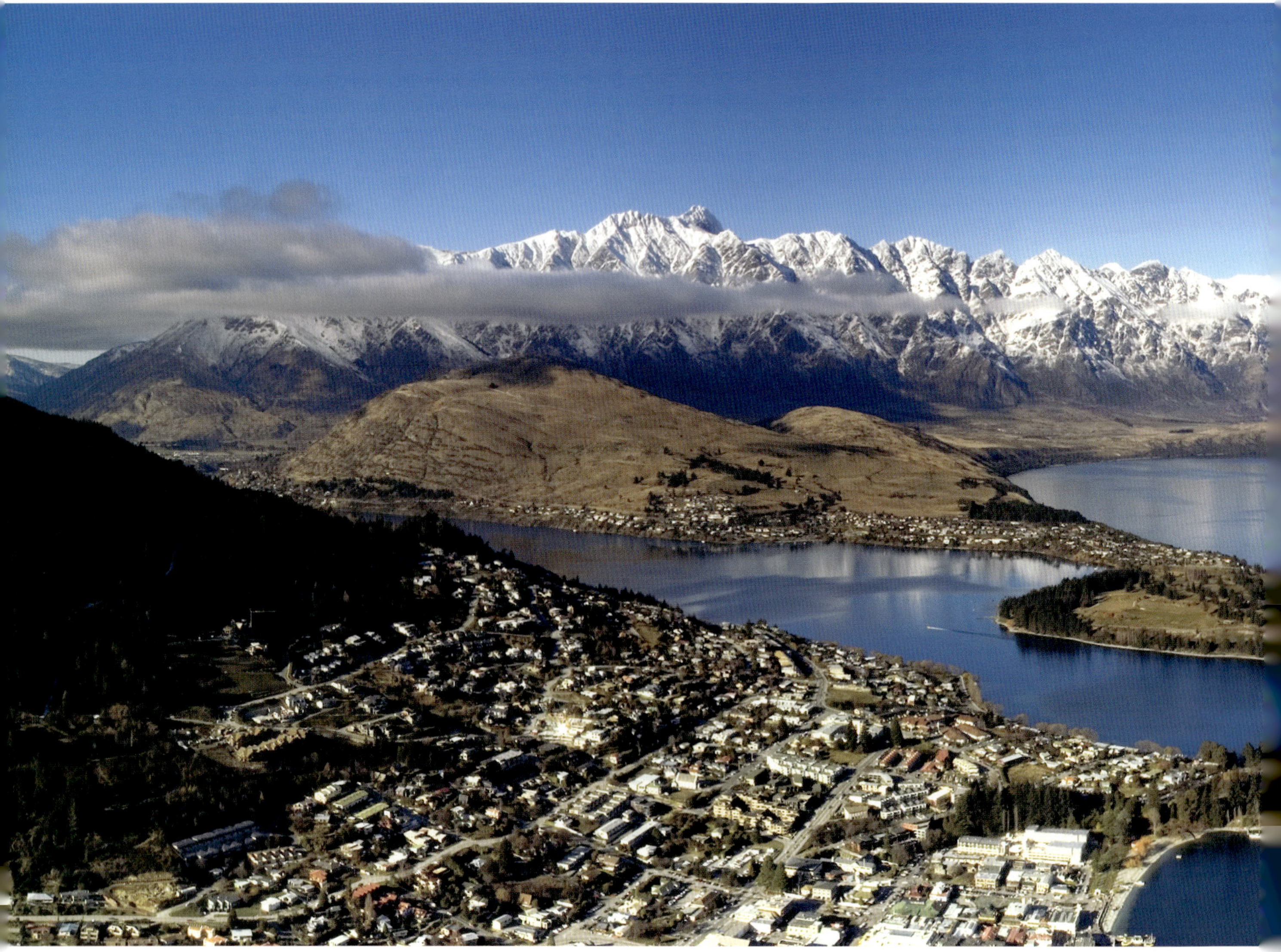

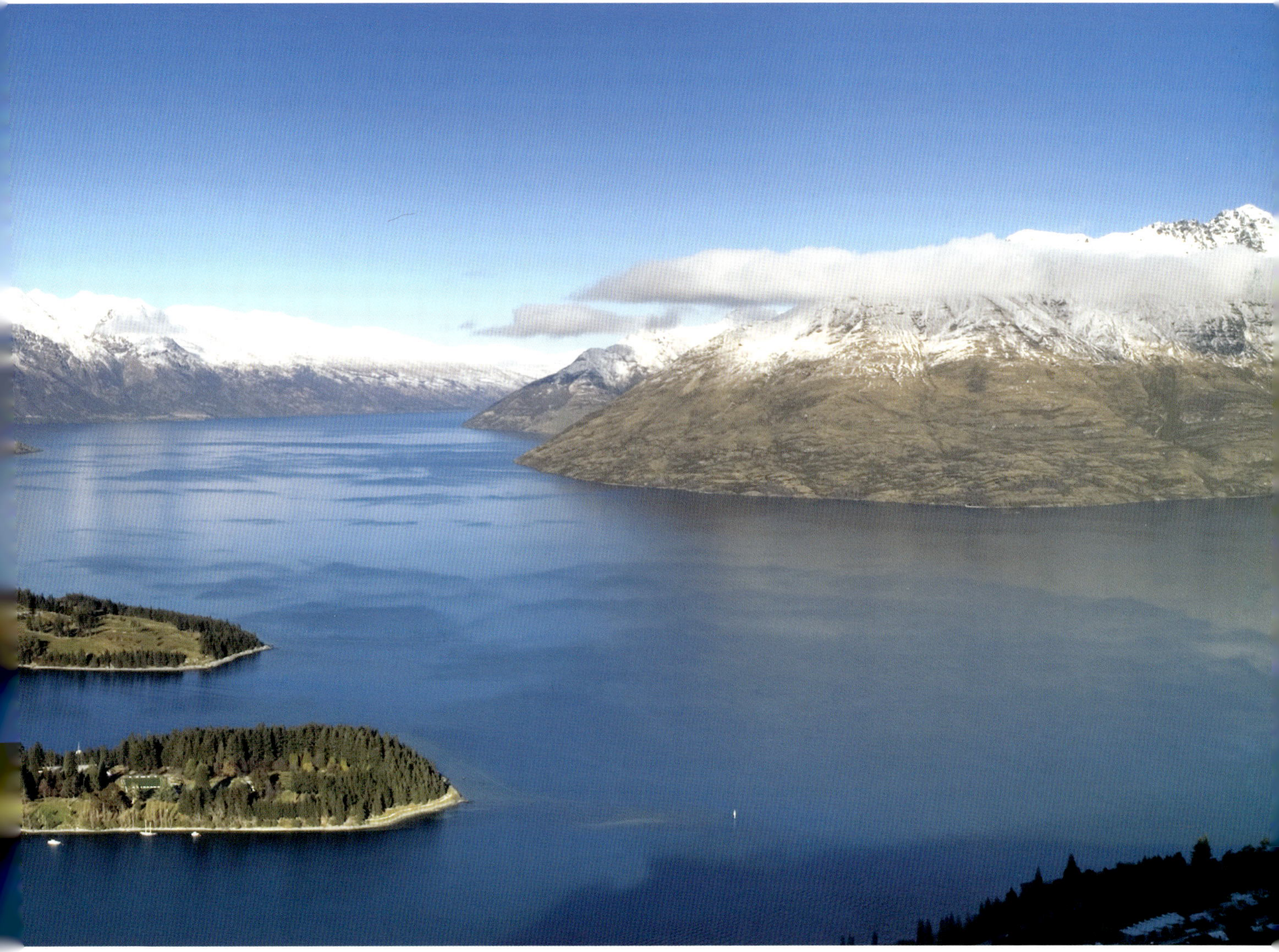

Glenorchy
Skippers Canyon
Coronet Peak Ski Area
Arrowtown
Lake Hayes
Gibbston
Frankton
Queenstown
Remarkables Ski Area
Walter Peak Station

Queenstown is a spectacular alpine resort on the shores of Lake Wakatipu in the heart of New Zealand's Southern Lakes region.

The town first made its mark internationally during the 1860s goldrush when thousands of prospectors sought their fortunes on Queenstown's lucrative goldfields. Queenstown was launched and today close to 2,000,000 people from all over the world visit every year.

Renowned for its outstanding scenery, snowsports, adrenalin activities, outdoor pursuits and growing arts and cultural awareness, Queenstown is a sophisticated and cosmopolitan all-year-round resort with distinctive changing seasons.

Development in Queenstown and the diverse Wakatipu Basin has always been intense and the resident population, attracted by the exceptional lifestyle, is one of the fastest growing in New Zealand. The colourful and innovative community has a strong commitment to Queenstown's future as New Zealand's foremost international tourist destination.

Queenstown at dusk

queenstown

Queenstown is made to measure for tourism.

It is a far cry today from the quiet holiday spot of the 1940s but change was inevitable. In its stunning environment stacked with scenic attractions, the resort is New Zealand's top international tourist destination attracting around 1,900,000 visitors a year.

Queenstown's growth has been a natural progression. Although the first steps were fragmented, by the early 1960s the direction was clear. Tourism was undoubtedly the town's bread and butter.

Today the resort is still a small town of around 15,000 residents. But it is one of the fastest growing places in New Zealand and the numbers are rapidly increasing with people from all over the world drawn to the tourism and lifestyle opportunities Queenstown offers.

While the tourism industry drives Queenstown development of infrastructure has over the years placed a heavy burden on ratepayers. Visitors now swell the population to over 30,000 a day at peak times calling for extensive and costly services to meet the demand.

A sewerage and water scheme installed in the early 1970s was funded by just 750 ratepayers. While the new scheme lifted an earlier ban on commercial building, the subsequent flurry of hotel and motel development was at a high price for Queenstown locals.

Eventually the Government helped by releasing Commonage land, high on Queenstown Hill overlooking the town, to generate funds for the scheme. Sites in the blue chip subdivision have attracted some of the highest real estate prices in the district.

The proceeds from the 40 hectare (100 acres) Commonage development have played a major role in funding Queenstown's ongoing infrastructure requirements.

Queenstown people epitomise the Kiwi 'do-it-yourself' attitude. The development of tourism attractions and facilities reflects the entrepreneurial nature of the town. Today there are several hundred sightseeing and adventure activities, many unique to Queenstown.

The Skyline Gondola cableway is an early success story and carries thousands of people to the spectacular viewing area at the top of Bob's Peak. The gondola was installed in 1967 and has undergone several upgrades and a luge now operates in tandem with the venture.

Left: Skyline Gondola   Right: Queenstown Winter Festival fireworks

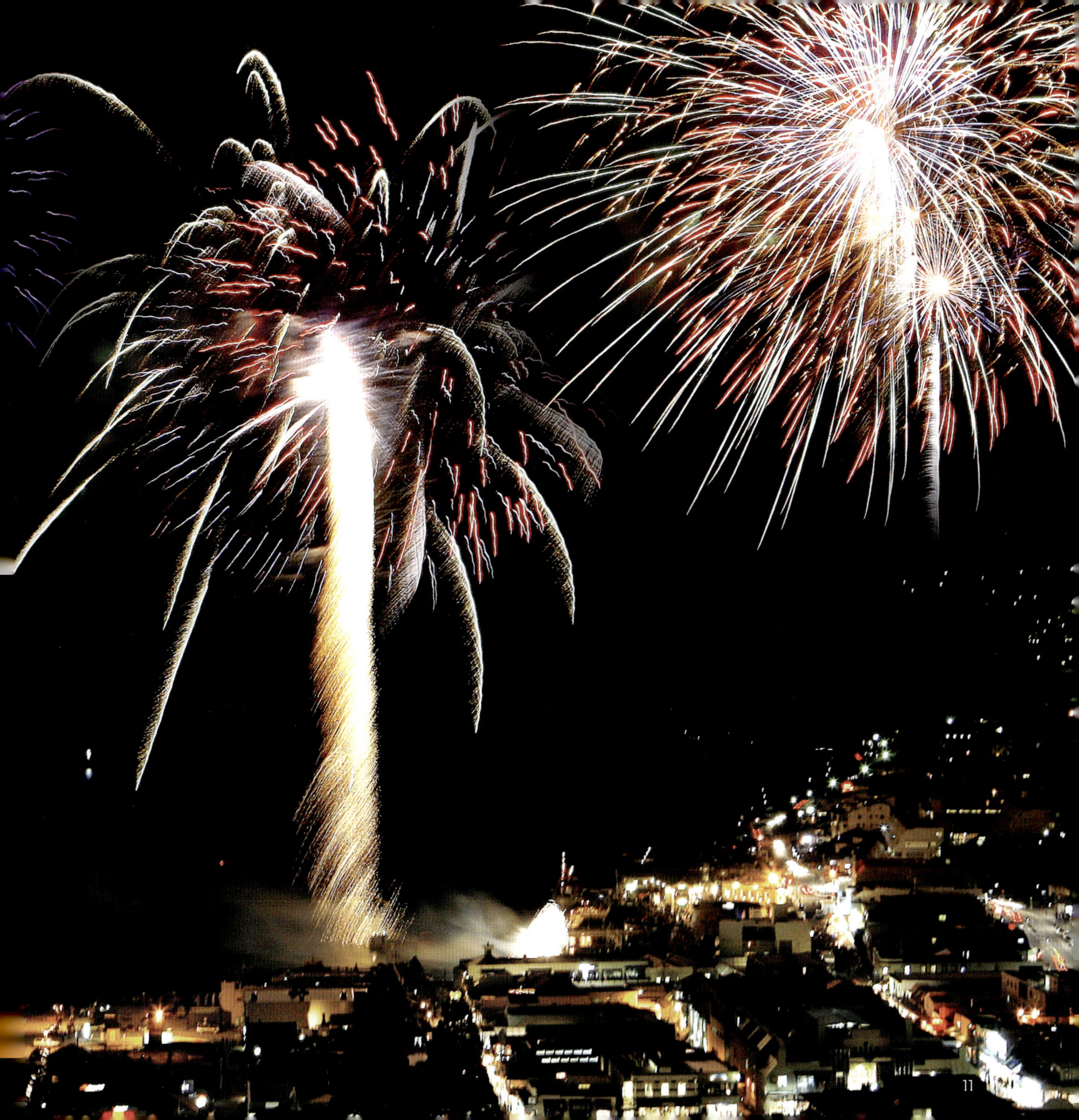

environment

While the Skyline gondola was the last word in progress in the 1960s it might not be so easy to develop the same piece of reserve land today. Queenstown welcomes development but not at any cost and an active environmental lobby closely watches what is happening. Their record shows they will fight hard to protect and preserve Queenstown's assets.

A proposed aerial cableway across Lake Wakatipu, a major tourist hotel on reserve land and helicopter landing pads close to the resort have all received the thumbs down at different times.

In a bid to save the Queenstown waterfront from overdevelopment in 1994, thousands of New Zealanders tried to prevent commercial expansion on a key Queenstown Bay reserve, previously owned by the New Zealand Railways Department. While the battle was lost and the Steamer Wharf complex was built a clear message had been sent to future developers.

The 1990s heralded the introduction of the Resource Management Act - legislation with the power to impose strict controls to protect the environment and reinforce the commitment of Queenstown's watchdogs.

Lake Wakatipu

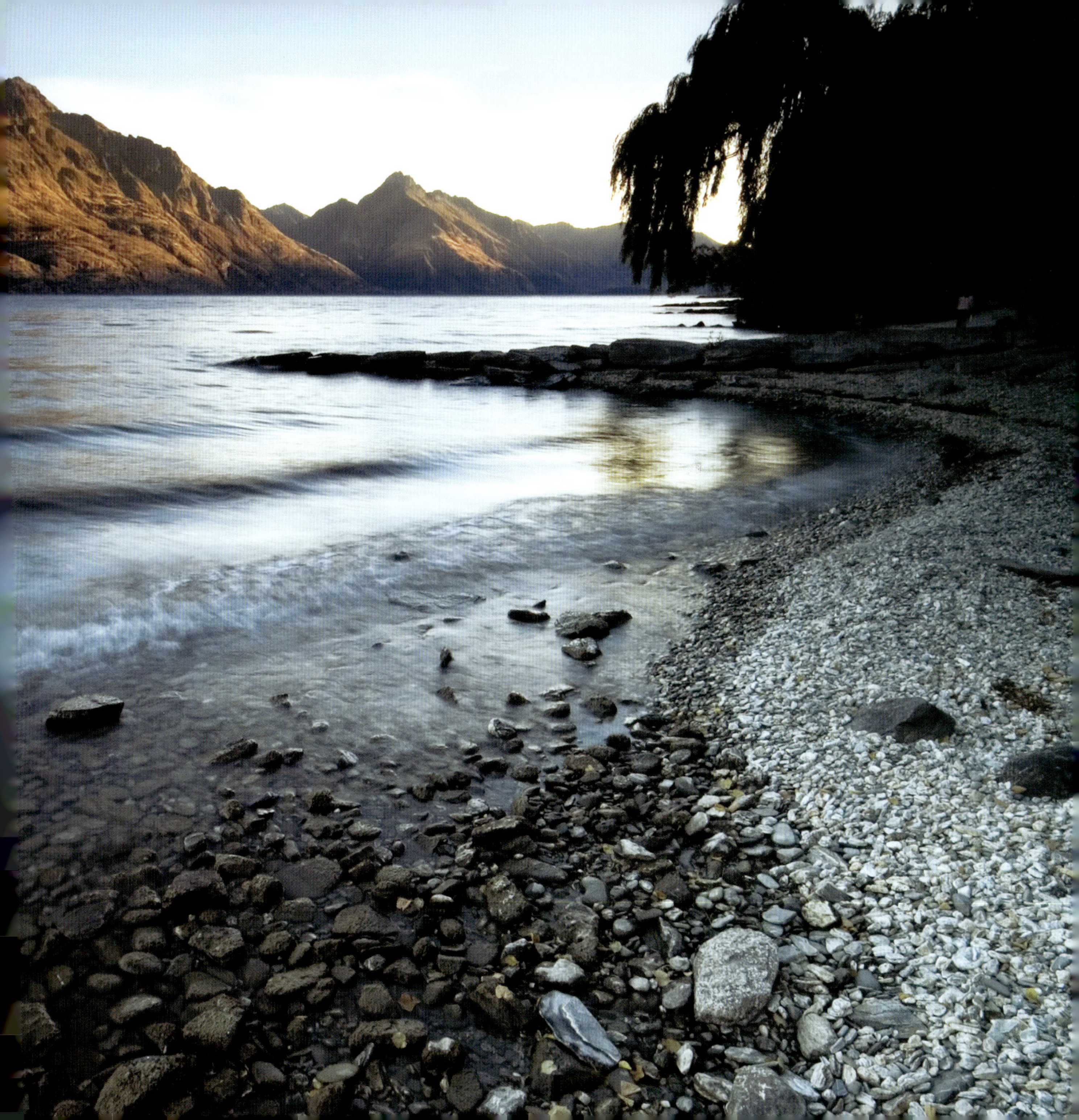

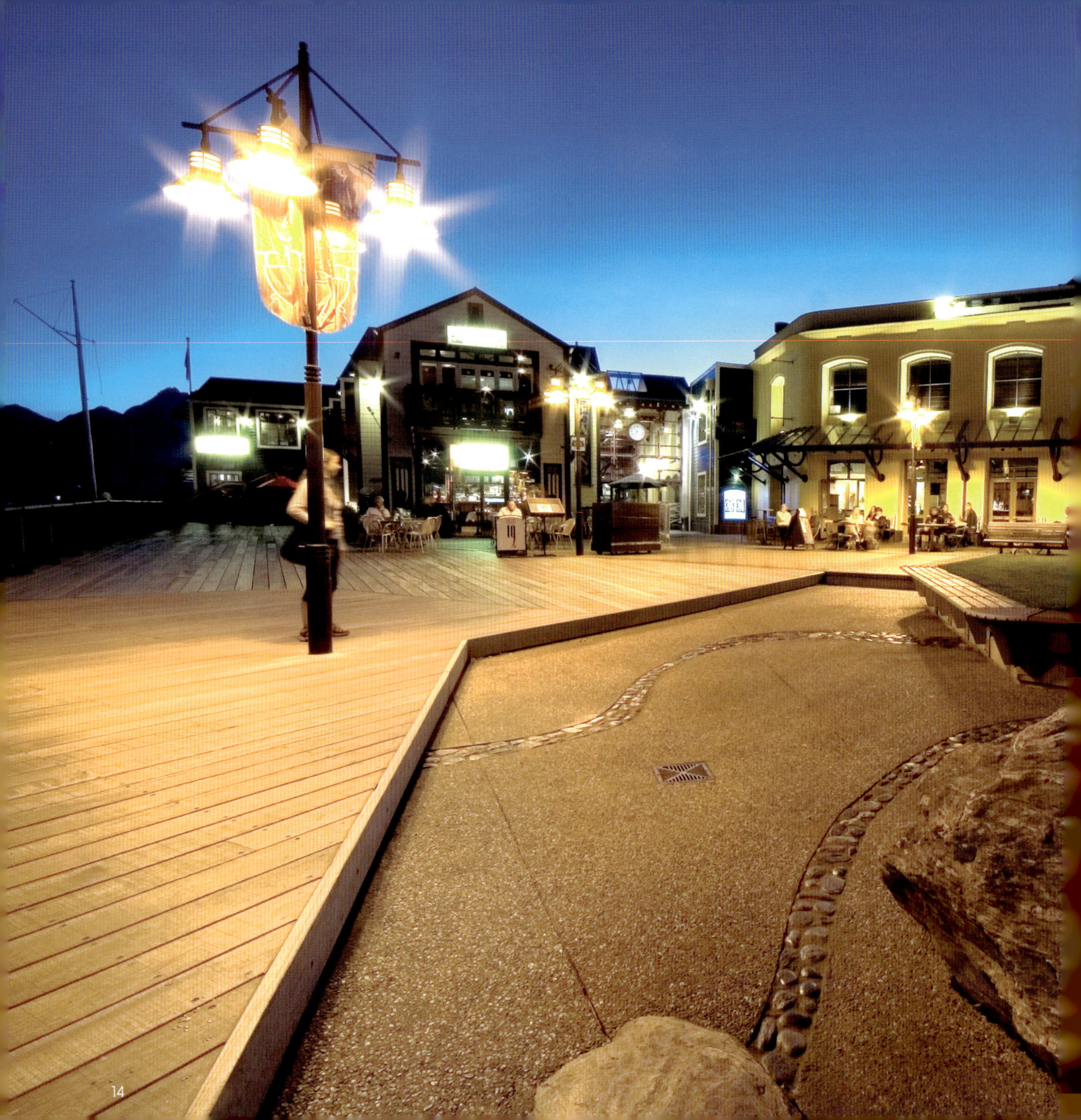

planning

In the mid-1980s Tourism Minister Mike Moore claimed tourism was one of the few industries New Zealand was "doing right." But he was concerned that the "problem in Queenstown is to do it right without spoiling the goods." A key point which is continually debated as decision makers grapple with managing growth.

Traditionally Queenstown and the surrounding area was controlled by both the Queenstown Borough Council and the Lake County Council. In 1986 local government reshuffling linked the two authorities to create the Queenstown Lakes District Council.

It was a new regime and the first item on the agenda was to change the system for funding costly tourism services. The council tried but failed to persuade the Government to impose a tourist tax. They did the next best thing and revamped the town's rating system so that the tourist industry, particularly the accommodation sector, pays the larger share of the rates bill.

Planning has also gone through major change since the first district scheme in 1970 targeted farmers. The reviewed scheme five years later was tourism - oriented putting controls in place for new development.

There was a clear-cut anti high-rise building policy and the 12 metre (36 feet) height limit downtown protects views and privacy although it is tested from time to time.

Sound strategic planning is vital to Queenstown's future. While progress is predictable the community argues for balance rather than unplanned growth to preserve the resort's assets.

Left: Steamer Wharf   Right: Queenstown Gardens

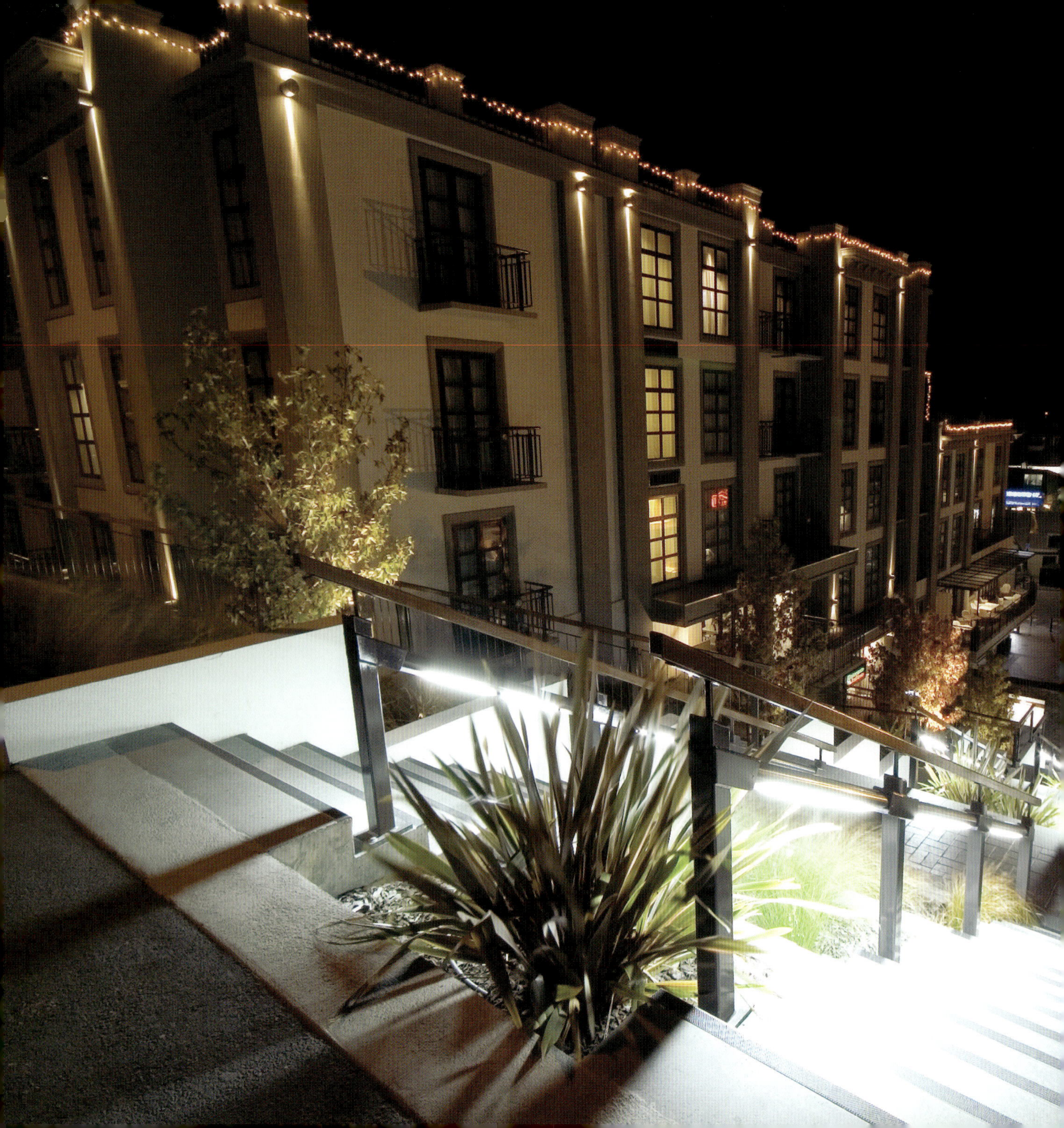

boom

Motel and hotel accommodation mushroomed in the early 1970s but the tourist industry hit a trough when the traditional Australian market declined. Things did not recover significantly until the boom of 1984 which was mainly driven by growth in the North American and Japanese markets.

New Zealand and overseas investors descended on Queenstown snapping up property for record prices. The boom was followed by a crash which held up some accommodation development. But in spite of this tourist rooms available in Queenstown had almost doubled to 2000 by the end of 1987.

Twenty years on there are over 100 commercial properties providing an extensive range of accommodation from the five star Sofitel and Hilton Hotels to backpacker hostels.

In the early 1990s there was a resurgence in investment in Queenstown notably by Asian investors and all the main hotels in the resort moved into Asian ownership. An improved outlook as the economy picked up, combined with predictions of a significant increase in tourist numbers, created a wave of confidence which has continued into the new century.

Growth in the retail and restaurant sectors has kept pace and Queenstown's commercial centre is constantly undergoing change. It began in the 1980s when the landmark historic O'Connells Hotel was demolished to make way for a modern shopping complex with the town's first escalators.

The Steamer Wharf Village on the waterfront opened several years later with cosmopolitan bars, restaurants and a casino. A controversial and bitter campaign was fought by Queenstown people, backed by support from throughout the country, to keep the resort casino-free. But approval was eventually given for two facilities with the second also opening in downtown Queenstown.

Central Queenstown has been redeveloped to create a sophisticated shopping and nightlife centre. Some long term local retailers have relocated to new developments on Queenstown's boundaries while national chains have moved into the town centre where there is no closing time. A Queenstown-wide exemption to open 24 hours a day 365 days a year is tailored for tourist shopping.

Restaurants have an international flavour. Of the 120 plus outlets food ranges from traditional Kiwi to Italian, Chinese, Japanese, Thai, Indian, French and Lebanese.

Sofitel Queenstown

locals

The pace of development in Queenstown has been dictated by the demands of tourism but what of community demands?

While most local residents rely one way or another on tourism there have been inevitable social consequences.

Inadequate accommodation has been an ongoing issue, surfacing during the 1986 boom, with high rents and little available low cost housing putting pressure on young people and families. It is still an issue today and affordable housing is continually flagged as a priority for the long-term growth of the local economy. The local authority has carried out in-depth research and is encouraging developers to provide affordable home sites across the district.

The goal is to create a stable Queenstown workforce and many of the town's employees are now living in the peripheral areas of Kingston, Lumsden, Cromwell and Glenorchy. The tourist industry is bolstered by young internationals on working holidays from South America, UK, Ireland, Europe, USA and Australia who add to the resort's cosmopolitan flair.

A lack of adequate care facilities has taken its toll on the town's elderly population. Many have had to move to other centres and there are continuous calls for change so that older local residents can remain in Queenstown.

Queenstown has an increasing focus on the arts and the internationally acclaimed Michael Hill Violin Concert stages its competition in the resort every two years. A multimillion dollar upgrade of a local art facility is planned and investigations are being made into building a regionally significant convention centre.

The tourism industry and the community is benefiting from the opening in 2006 of New Zealand's first resort education institute. Queenstown Resort College's aim is to provide professionally trained staff to meet the projected national tourist and hospitality employment shortage. Students from throughout New Zealand and overseas are studying at the purpose built facility in the heart of Central Queenstown.

Left: Searle Lane & Social Bar and Restaurant
Right: Long-term resident the late Paddy Mathias

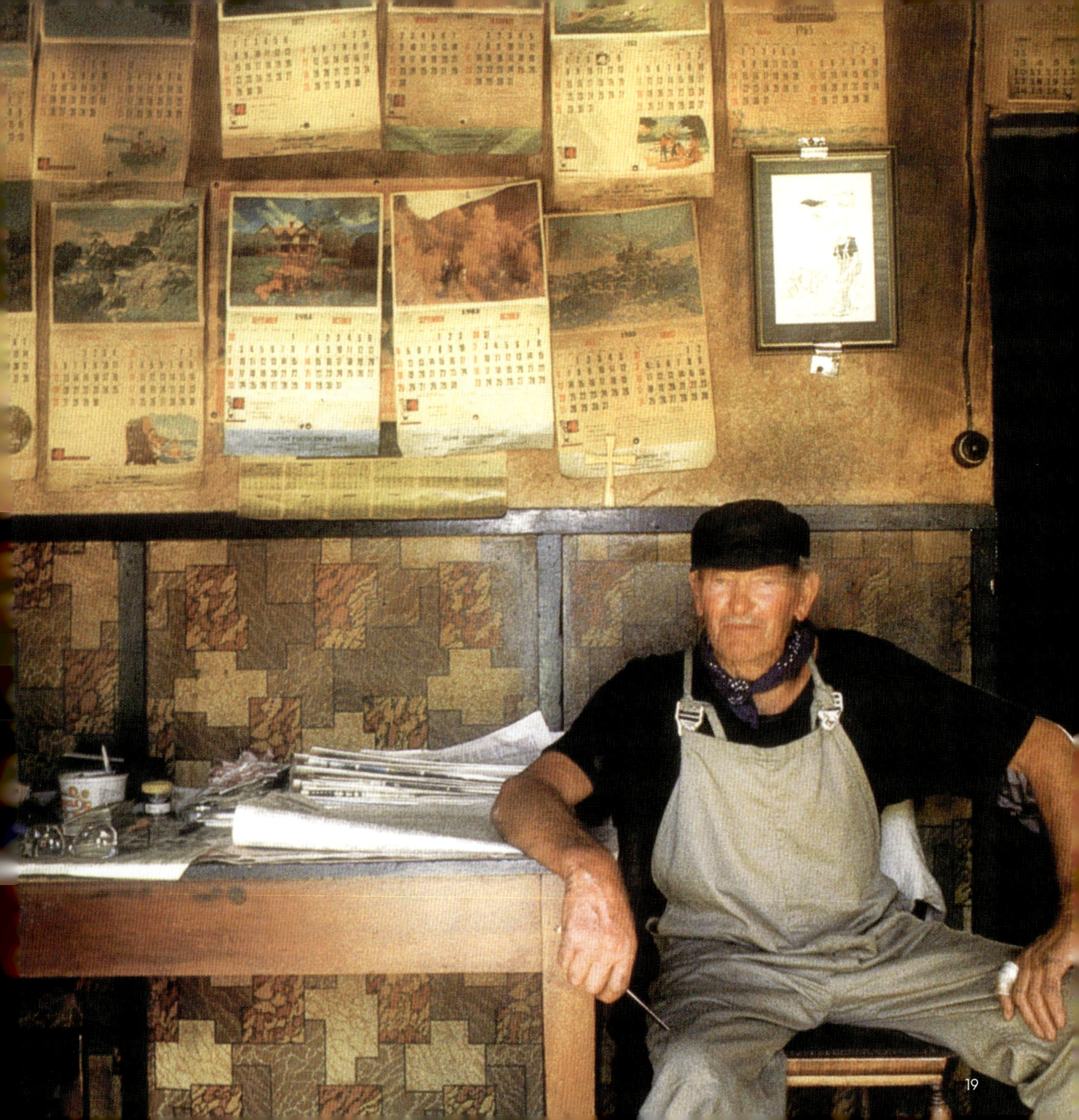

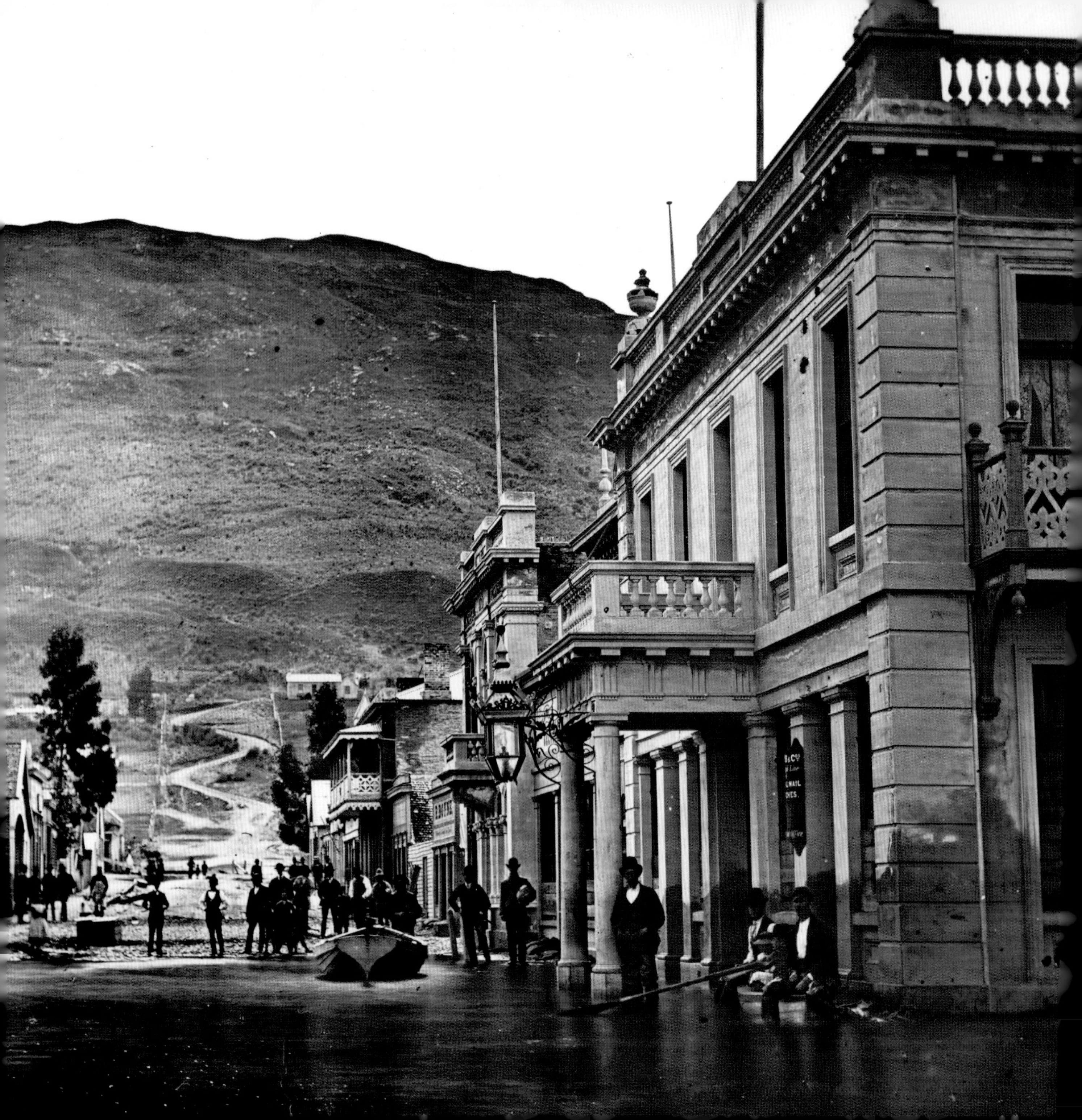

early queenstown

Although Queenstown's history is linked with gold the trailblazers were men of the soil.

William Gilbert Rees and Nicholas Von Tunzelman arrived first in the early 1860s and took up large tracts of land around the Wakatipu.

Rees initially settled in Queenstown Bay after apparently winning it in the toss of a coin with Von Tunzelman. As loser Von Tunzelman took a 20,000 hectare (50,000 acres) property on the western side of the lake.

The Rees property was a stark piece of country covered in thorny matagouri and sharp-bladed speargrass. He set up a simple base and had the place to himself until gold was discovered in 1862 and miners converged from all over the world. Entrepreneurs arrived to service the Wakatipu goldfields, and buildings mainly of calico and wood, went up at an incredible rate creating the town's first commercial development boom.

Pubs, eating houses and commercial buildings formed the hub of the township and a public meeting in 1863 changed its name from "The Camp" to Queenstown - "a town fit for a queen."

There are plenty of reminders of those early days. Ballarat Street, now the Queenstown Mall, is lined with original properties restored and converted to modern day use. Marine Parade is the last remaining precinct of original houses intact in Queenstown. It includes the Williams Cottage the town's oldest building built in 1864, the Masonic Lodge and the Archer Cottage.

The original McNeill Cottage has been restored and operates as a boutique brewery and bar.

Left: Ballarat Street - 1878 flood   Right: Queenstown c.1880

Attempts to move the Williams Cottage in the 1990s caused a public outcry. The Queenstown Lakes District Council and the Queenstown Heritage Trust joined forces to purchase and safeguard the building. The cottage has been preserved and converted to a café and design store. A heritage order has also been imposed on the next door Archer Cottage.

While there had been moves in the 1960s to introduce a special building code to retain Queenstown's 19th century character the theme was considered more appropriate for Arrowtown.

It may be too late for some relics like the Buckhams Brewery stone malthouse which was bulldozed down to make way for the Novotel Gardens Hotel on the lakeshore, but there is an awareness today of the importance of retaining and preserving the district's heritage.

The New Zealand Historic Places Trust and the Queenstown Historical Society act as custodians, pressuring authorities to preserve and conserve early assets. Not just buildings but anything with a history - even stone bridges and trees - are now protected through the district scheme.

Below: Williams Cottage built in 1864   Right: Williams Cottage today

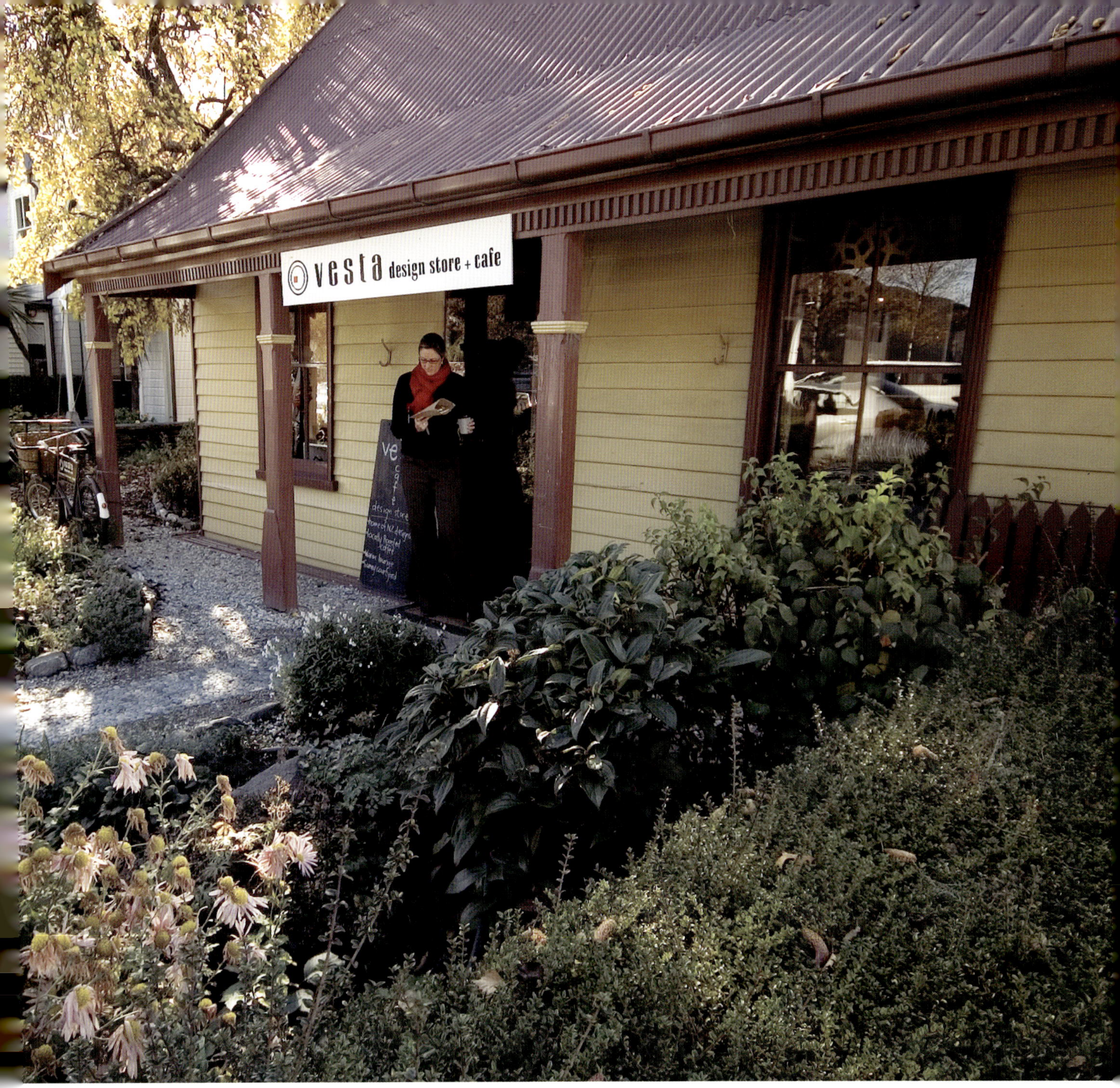
vesta design store + cafe

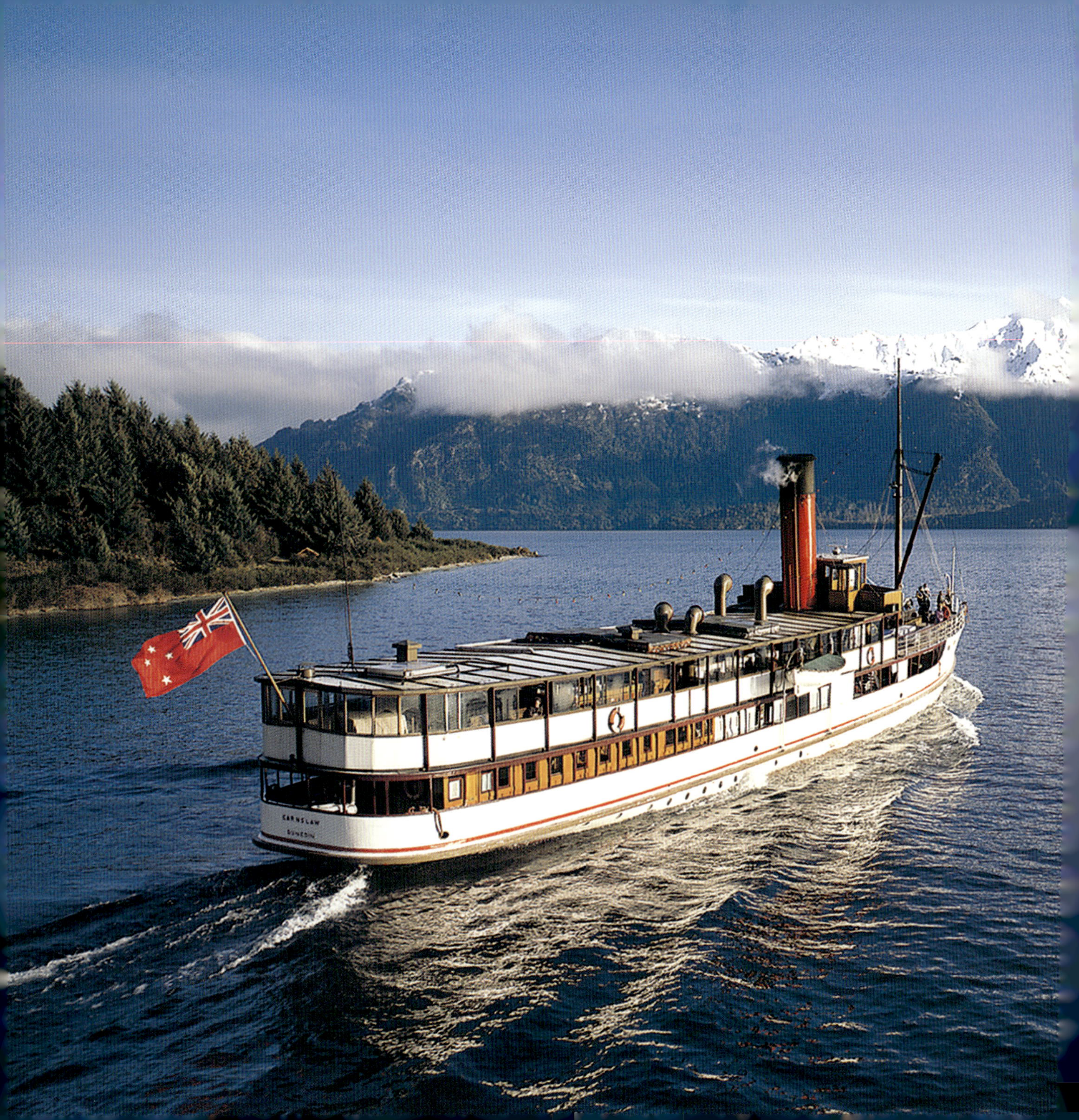
EARNSLAW

lake wakatipu

First and foremost Lake Wakatipu is a recreational lake but 150 years ago, it was anything but.

The demands of the goldrush and farming called for transport and in the 1860s there were about 30 steamers and sailing ships working on the lake. Essential items had to be carried from Kingston at the south end of the lake and there was no road access until 1936. Romantically named vessels such as Wild Irish Girl, The Nugget and Young American delivered supplies to the goldfields and the farming settlements around the lake.

By the turn of the century there were only three steamships left on the lake - the Ben Lomond, the Mountaineer and the Antrim - all now part of Lake Wakatipu's legend.

During the latter half of the 19th century a train service which lasted until 1979 operated to Kingston at the south end of the lake. It was a strategic port and boats connected with the train, picking up supplies for the goldfields and lakeside farms.

In the early 1900s the New Zealand Railways Department took over private shipping on the lake. Its flagship was the twin-screw steamer Earnslaw which was launched at Kingston in 1912 and operated freight, mail and passenger services on Lake Wakatipu.

Even then the "Grand Old Lady of the Lake" was something of an anachronism with the steam age on the decline. But she was built to survive and continued to compete with road transport after the opening of the Kingston to Queenstown road in the 1920s. However when the Queenstown to Glenorchy road opened in 1962 the writing was on the wall. The Earnslaw was declared uneconomic in 1968 and a national protest at her potential scuttling led to her being sold to private enterprise.

TSS Earnslaw

26

It was the end of an era for the old steamer but her new owners, Fiordland Travel, now operating as Real Journeys, have maintained her in stately style and there are few visitors who leave Queenstown without taking an Earnslaw cruise. She is a New Zealand tourist icon and one of the last remaining coal fired vessels in the Southern Hemisphere.

The old Kingston steam train, which became obsolete as a freight train in 1979 was preserved and until 2009 operated tourist excursions between Kingston and nearby Fairlight There are plans by a private investor to relaunch the Kingston Flyer venture.

The Kingston-Queenstown road owes its beginnings to a disastrous dam project on the Kawarau River at the outlet of Lake Wakatipu. A structure, which later became a traffic bridge across the river, was built as a novel mining dam by the Kawarau Mining Company in a bid to dry up the river and recover huge quantities of gold, believed to be in the river bed. In September 1926 the great day came. The crowds gathered and the dam gates were shut but there was no sign of the gold-laden river bed. While the lake waters were trapped in, the backflow from the Shotover and Arrow rivers prevented the river bed being exposed and the project was a complete failure.

But the Kawarau Falls bridge has been a bonus for tourist operators and a highlight of a Kawarau Jet excursion is to skim across the rapids at the outlet. The bridge itself is under severe pressure and detailed investigations for a replacement two lane bridge to relieve the congestion are underway.

Left: The Mountaineer c.1910   Right: Kawarau Jet

wakatipu today

Lake Wakatipu is New Zealand's third largest lake and probably one of the coldest. It is 84 kilometres long (52 miles) and around 3.5 kilometres (two miles) wide.

There is an unusual rise and fall effect in the lake. According to Maori legend it is the heart of a giant, who kidnapped a Maori chief's daughter and was killed by a warrior, beating beneath the surface. However scientific explanations relate it to atmospheric pressure and the wind.

Flooding is an issue and in the last major flood in 1999 Lake Wakatipu rose to its highest level in more than 100 years. Central Queenstown was inundated by lake water creating a civil emergency. There is ongoing debate on the best methods of flood protection for the town.

Several rivers feed the lake but its only outlet is the Kawarau. The spectacular river is an important recreational playground and in the early 1980s environmentalists spearheaded nationwide support to prevent any possible damming of the Kawarau River for hydroelectric power.

A petition, capturing the interest of tourists as well as New Zealanders, was signed by more than 2000 people and in 1985 the Government agreed to protect the Kawarau as a wild and scenic river. Nine years later a national conservation order provided further protection for the river and its tributaries.

Every conceivable craft scuds across Lake Wakatipu these days. It's an obvious target for tourist ventures operating lake cruises, jetbikes, parasailing, windsurfers and kayaks.

Yachting is a popular Queenstown pastime and the Wakatipu Yacht Club's annual event, the Donald Hay race, charts the course from Kingston to Queenstown set by this early explorer.

The commercial heart of Queenstown nestles into Queenstown Bay where boat trips operate from jetties along the foreshore.

The main pier is home for the Queenstown Underwater World, a glassed-in viewing room providing eyeball-to-eyeball contact with wild trout, eels and ducks.

Fishing is not allowed in Queenstown Bay but the rest of the lake has some fine trolling and the rivers that feed it offer superb fly fishing. The fishing season on Lake Wakatipu and the Kawarau River is open all year but the inflowing rivers are restricted to a shorter season.

Lake Wakatipu, like other waterways in the south, has been affected by the invasive freshwater algae didymo which attaches itself to rocks. Its spread is being closely monitored but there is no threat to swimming or tourist operations in Queenstown Bay.

Fishing in Lake Wakatipu

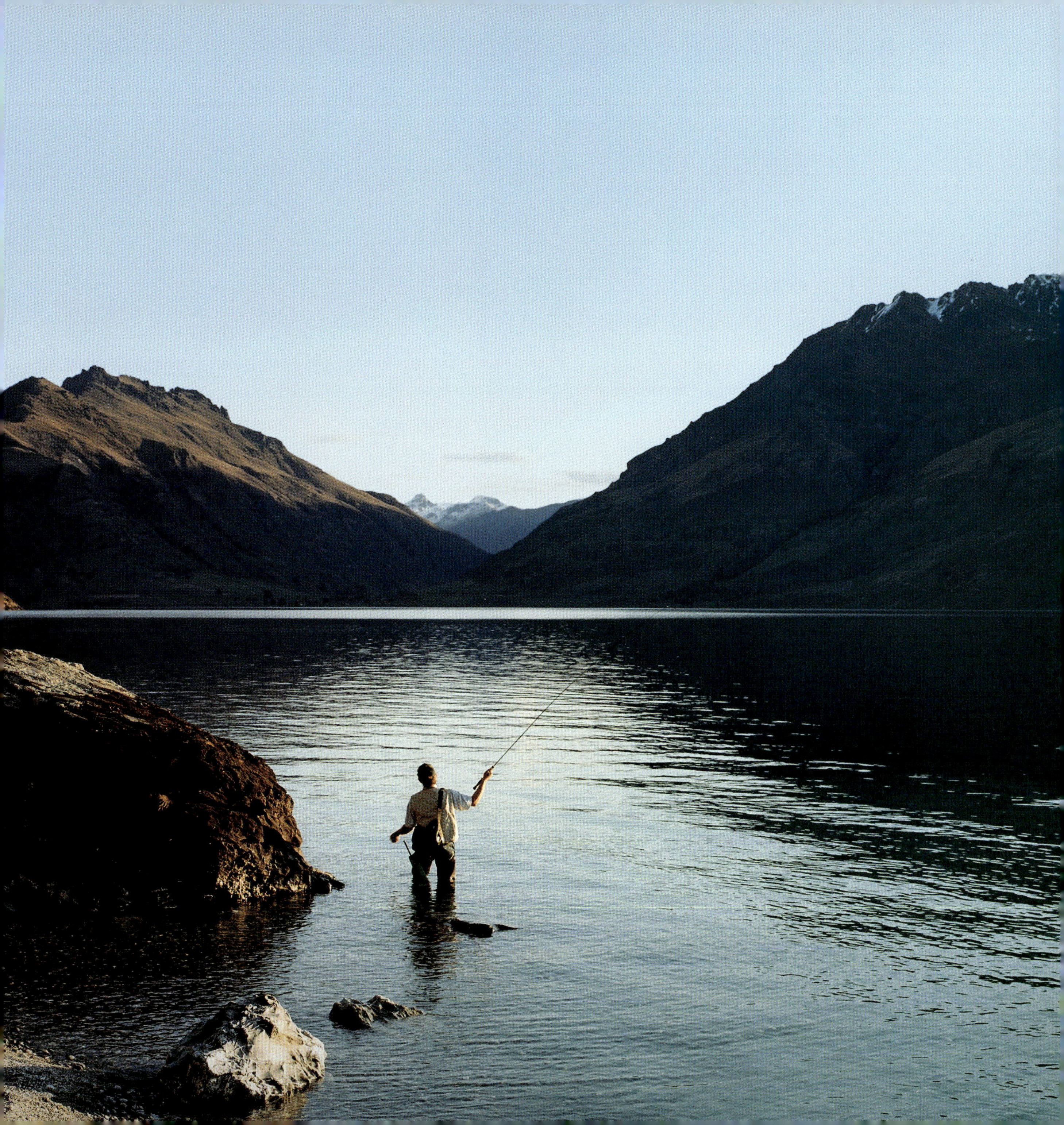

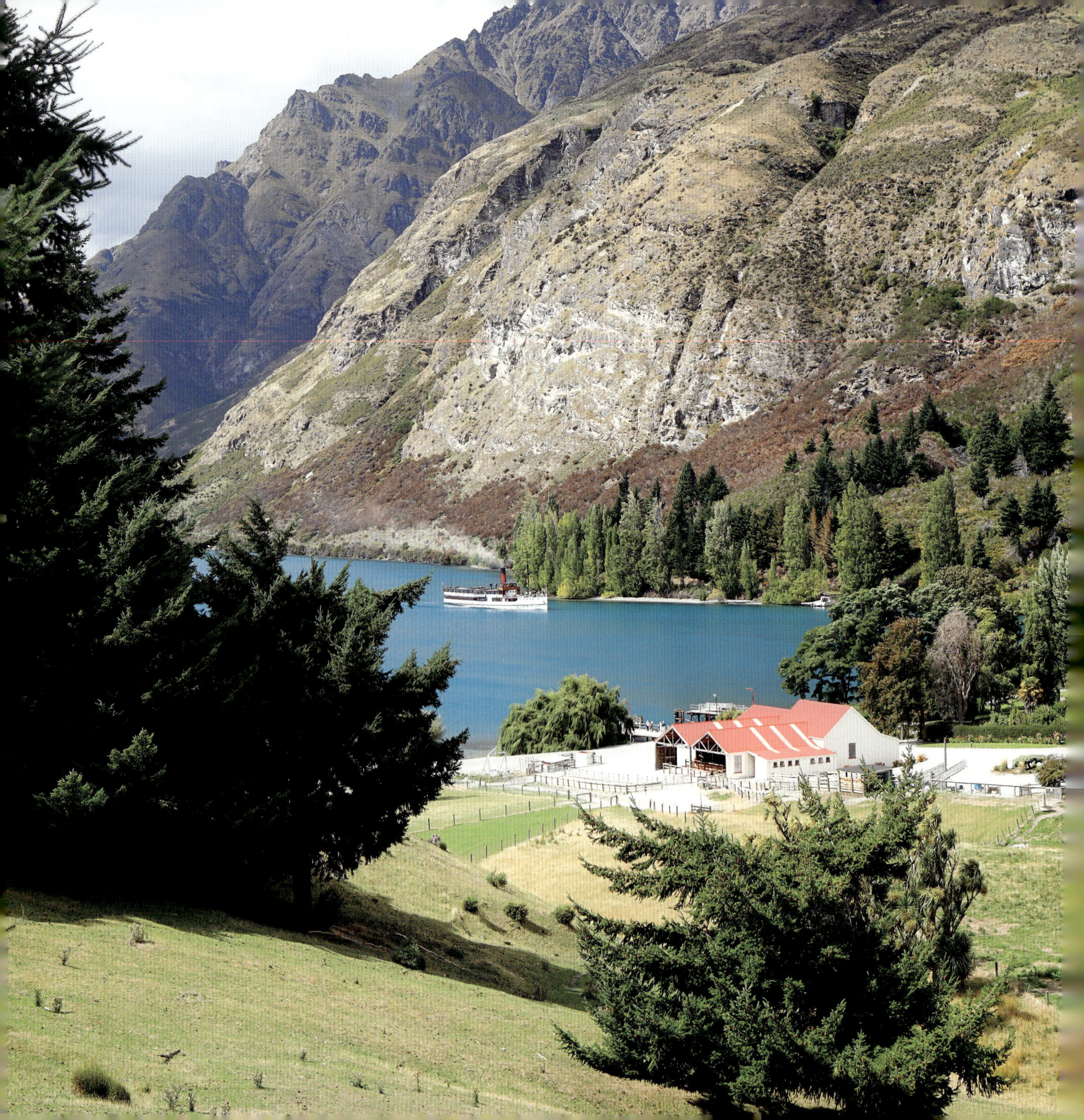

lakeside stations

Lake Wakatipu's high country sheep and cattle stations are in a world of their own - remote, rugged and independent.

The pioneering families who settled the stations have a special place in the district's history and while today farming is still the backbone of most properties, some have diversified into tourism.

Cecil Peak Station ran an early tourist operation in the 1960s spearheaded by former RAF bomber pilot Popeye Lucas and his wife Lorie. First they rented out shearers quarters and small cottages on the 13,770 hectare (34,425 acre) property, then they promoted daily tourist trips from Queenstown.

The Lucases ran a thriving business at Cecil Peak, selling out in 1976 to an American company. Ten years on it was sold to the owners of the neighbouring Walter Peak Station who continued a tourist venture there. Today Cecil Peak is in overseas ownership and no longer involved in tourism.

Cecil Peak (1947 metres) and Walter Peak (1815 metres) are two of the region's most significant landmarks, named by Queenstown founder William Rees to recognise his son Cecil Walter Rees.

Walter Peak Station has always had a high profile and over the years several proposals have been floated to convert it into a fully-fledged destination resort.

In the late 1960s Englishman George Wiles bought the station and announced grandiose plans to turn the high country farming property into a tourist playground. He designed a village with 250 chalets, restaurants, shops and a nightclub.

Wiles started daily launch trips to the station from Queenstown and original homes on the property were converted into tourist attractions. The Colonel's House built by the first owner in 1907 was the centrepiece. It was set up as a museum but tragically was destroyed by fire in 1977. The house was rebuilt to the original design and now operates as a restaurant.

Wiles' big plans for Walter Peak never came off. Things fell apart when he attempted to float a public company and failed. He disappeared from the scene and in 1973 the Reid Development Company bought the property.

In 1985 North American investors joined forces with Reid but their plans for a tourist village were never realised. Five years later the property sold to a Singaporean consortium. Today Real Journeys operates daily Earnslaw cruises to Walter Peak, where visitors experience farm tours and farming hospitality.

Walter Peak Station

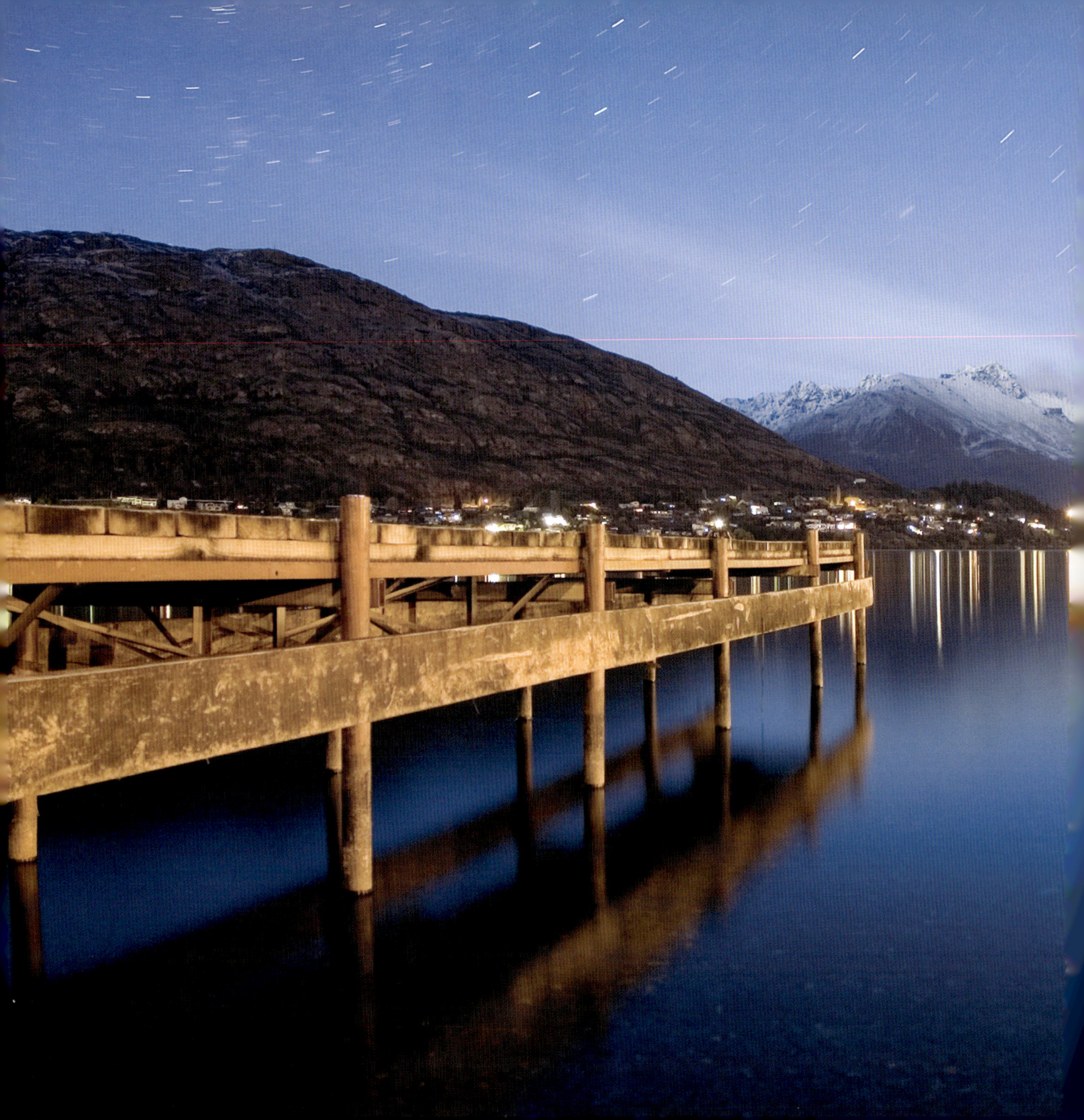

frankton

Frankton has moved into the 21st century as a key Wakatipu centre.

The settlement lost out to Queenstown in the 1870s when there was talk of putting the district's administration headquarters there. However the first Lakes District hospital was built in Frankton in 1863 and has remained in spite of attempts to move it to Queenstown. A new hospital was opened in the late 1980s and a range of medical services, including a home for the elderly, are housed under one roof.

The district's ambulance service relocated its base from Queenstown in 2001 building a $2 million complex alongside the hospital.

At the entrance to Queenstown Frankton was the ideal location for an airport. The Mount Cook Company pioneered air travel into Queenstown's alpine terrain and the original Frankton airstrip was lengthened in 1964 to cater for its DC3 service. Then came the Hawker Siddeley 748 aircraft linking Queenstown and Auckland in 1968.

The company's monopoly of the skies was broken in 1985 when Newmans Air, later to become Ansett New Zealand, arrived in Queenstown. Four years later the Whisper Jet, the British Aerospace 146, was flying into the resort - an environmentally acceptable option welcomed by Frankton residents.

Ansett New Zealand was subsequently taken over by Qantas whose subsidiary Jetstar now operates direct daily services to Auckland and Christchurch.

Mount Cook Airlines flies under the Air New Zealand banner and the airlines fought an acrimonious battle with locals over the introduction of Boeing 737 services to Queenstown. A compromise was reached and the jets, fitted with noise reducing hush-kits, made their debut into Queenstown in 1991.

Direct Trans-Tasman winter services were launched in 1995 heralding yet another milestone for the resort, flying skiers from Sydney and Brisbane. Today there are year-round direct services from Sydney, Brisbane and Melbourne boosting the Australian tourist market.

Frankton Beach

The increased services have demanded upgraded amenities and the Queenstown Airport has been expanded to create a contemporary terminal complex with international facilities.

Frankton has developed into a significant local shopping centre with many young families making their homes close by at Remarkables Park, Lake Hayes Estate and Quail Rise. Remarkables Park has attracted national chains along with well established local retail outlets. The proposed Five Mile Village will further expand commercial and retail facilities at Frankton.

The contemporary Kawarau Village on the original Kawarau Falls Stations site, established by William Rees in 1864, opened in mid-2011 housing the luxury Hilton Queenstown and the Hilton managed Kawarau Hotel. The internationally rated complex with its range of restaurants and bars is popular with locals and water taxis operate to and from Queenstown.

The $2 billion Jacks Point township. also close to Frankton, is capable of housing up to 5,000 people. Jacks Point is the largest single residential development in the history of the Queenstown Lakes District and incorporates an 18-hole championship golf course.

The ongoing growth in the area has led to increased community facilities at Frankton. Wakatipu's second kindergarten is based here and the state-of-the-art Remarkables Primary School has opened on the lakeshore.

The Queenstown Events Centre hosts local, national and international sporting events as well as large-scale conferences and trade shows. The construction of the neighbouring multi-million dollar aquatic centre was held up over a lengthy debate whether it should be sited in Frankton or Queenstown.

Frankton is a superb recreational area. A new boat marina is on the drawing board and the safe, sunny Frankton Arm beach explodes with activity in summer.

Walking and cycling tracks have been developed around the lake and the Frankton golf course is a popular nine hole option while the Queenstown Golf Club's Kelvin Heights Course offers a greater challenge amongst outstanding scenery.

Left: Frankton by night   Right: Hilton Queenstown

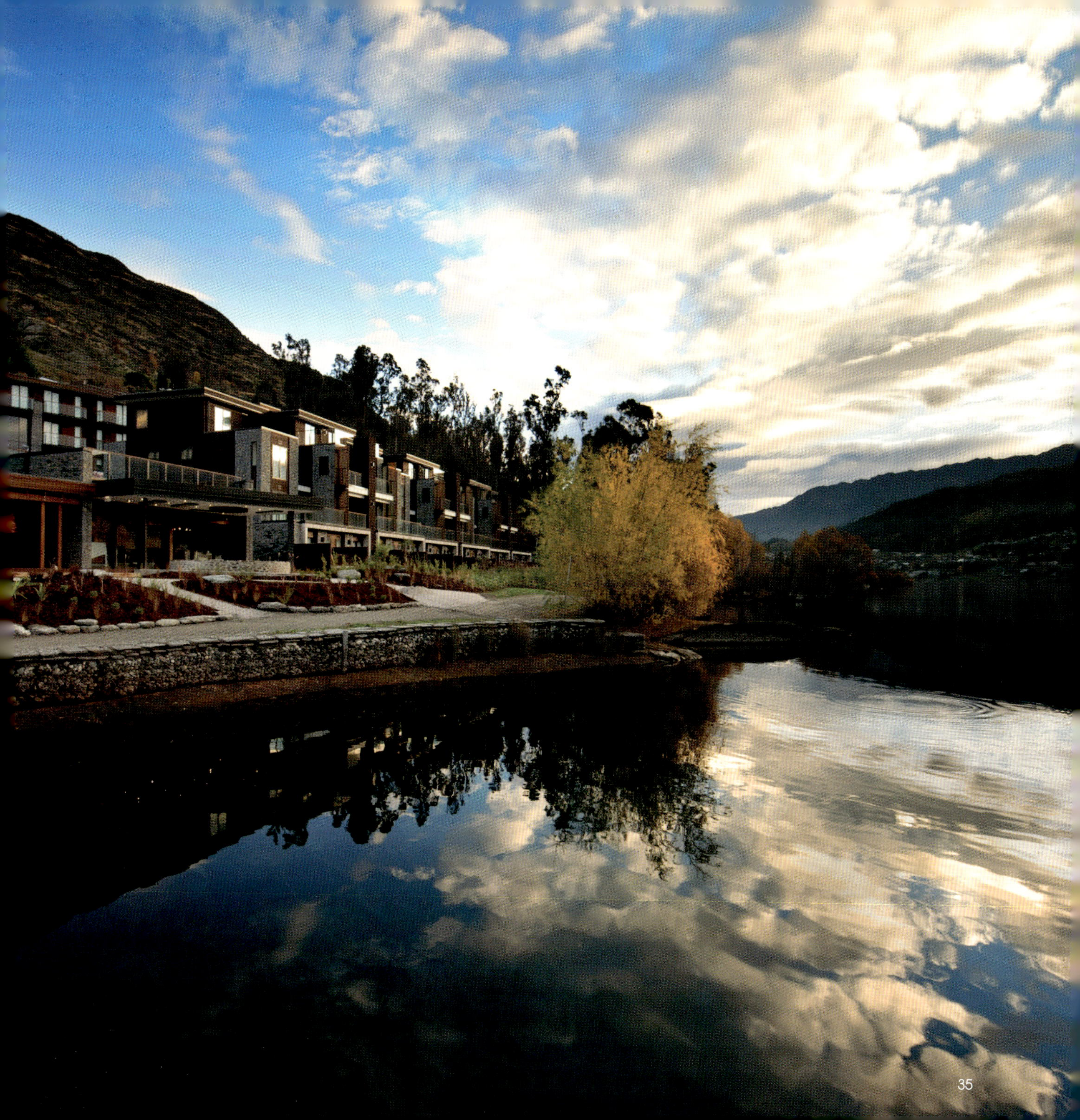

the shotover valley

In 1862 the Shotover River became the centre of New Zealand's largest gold rush thanks mainly to the exploits of a young shearer, Thomas Arthur, who struck gold while out on a Sunday jaunt.

Arthur never returned to the shearing shed. Lured by the gold, he and his partner are rumoured to have taken up to £4000 worth from the Shotover River in just two months.

The Shotover River was one of the richest gold bearing rivers in the world. At the height of the Shotover goldrush, there were around 3000 miners living in the region at Maori Point, Stoney Creek and Skippers.

Once the rush was over the miners left but Thomas Arthur's names lives on. Arthurs Point just six kilometres (3.6 miles) from Queenstown en route to the Coronet Peak Ski Area and Arrowtown is a popular residential settlement.

It was traditionally a hillside of holiday cribs but has expanded into a home for permanent residents. Across the Shotover River former farmland has been carved up for residential subdivision.

Long-time residents have made Arthurs Point their home over the years. Local identity, the late Paddy Mathias, lived for decades in a charming cottage with no telephone and only a copper to heat the bath water - in stark contrast to the modern hotels close by. The cottage has been listed as a heritage feature in the Queenstown Lakes district plan recognising its significance and providing it with permanent protection.

The Arthurs Point Hotel, built in 1862 to serve the goldfields, has now gone but was for many years the focal point of the community. Nearby Gantley's Restaurant, formerly known as Packers Arms, was once a welcome hotel stop for miners on the way to the diggings. After the goldrush the building became derelict until its renovation and new lease of life as a restaurant in the late 1960s.

Left: Sluicing in Skippers c.1890   Right: Shotover Valley

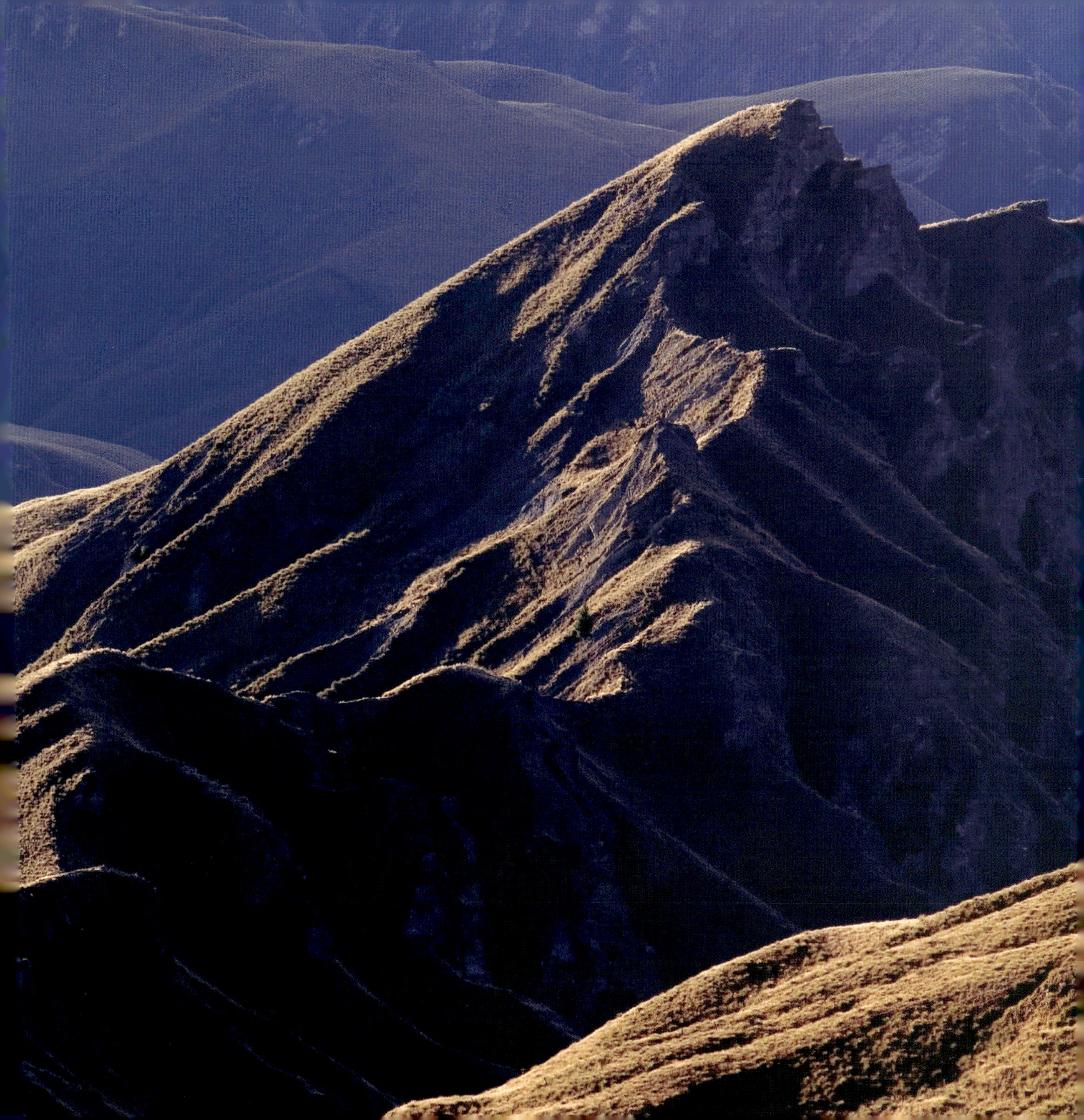

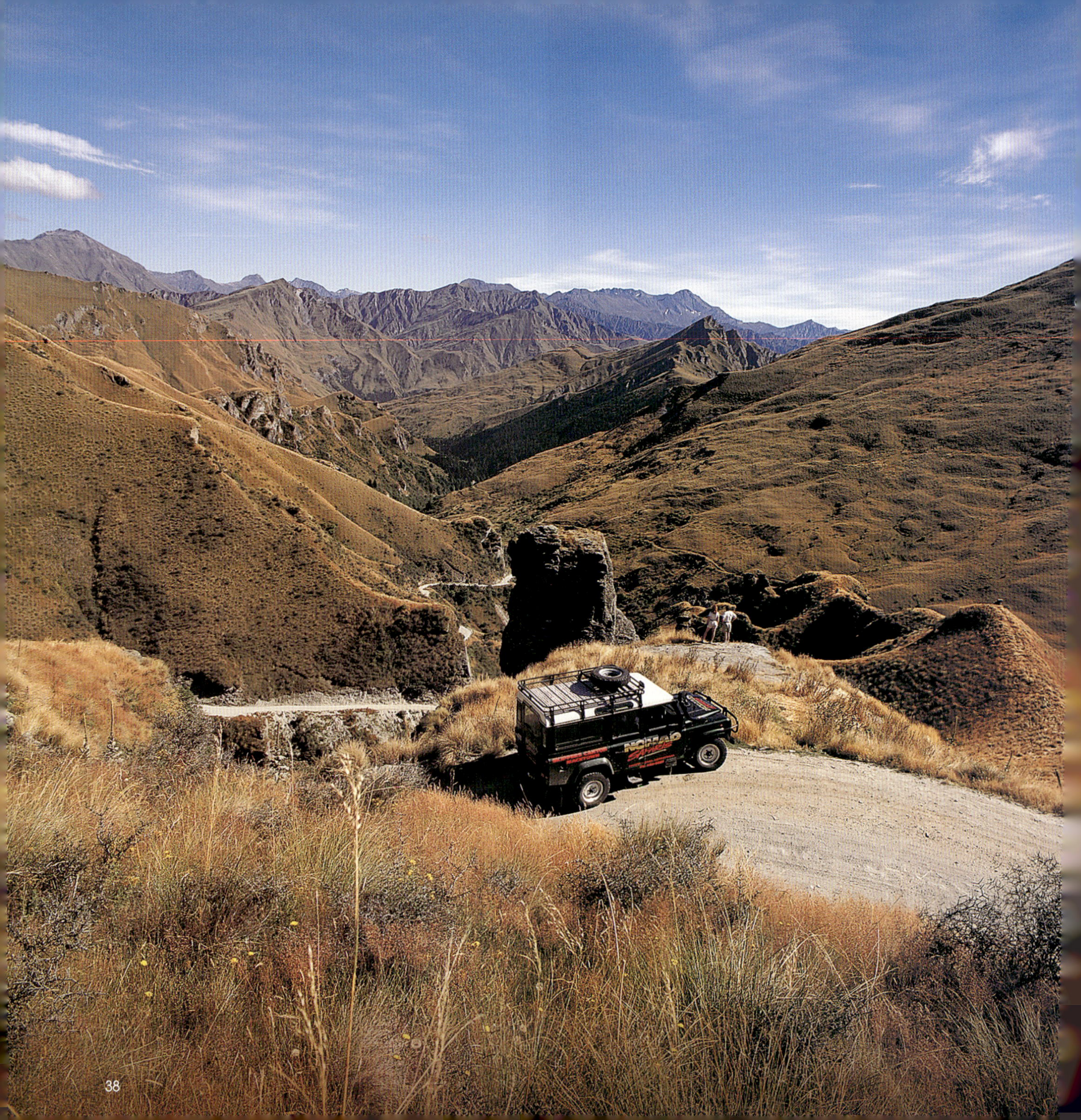
NOMAD

skippers canyon

Skippers Canyon is a flagship of the New Zealand tourism industry. People flock there to jet boat, raft, kayak, mountain bike, hike and explore the scenic and historic valley by 4WD vehicle.

This notable region was once the scene of frenetic mining activity. A permanent township of around 3000 people lived in Skippers during the goldrush. The pioneers and miners left their mark which tourist operators have capitalised on, and the once thriving town with its hotels and even a school, is the backdrop for today's adventure seekers.

The Skippers Road is an adventure in itself. The tortuous route provides a unique access, twisting and turning through scenic, mountainous country with sheer drops to the Shotover River below.

The road opened in 1890 replacing the narrow bridle track forged by the miners. It was a massive undertaking and is a memorial to the commitment of the early road builders. Horses and buggies were the first to use it - today the traffic is mainly tourist vehicles.

The Skippers Road has been registered as an historic item by both the Historic Places Trust and the Queenstown Lakes District Council recognising its place in the district's history.

Left: Skippers Road   Right: Skippers Suspension Bridge

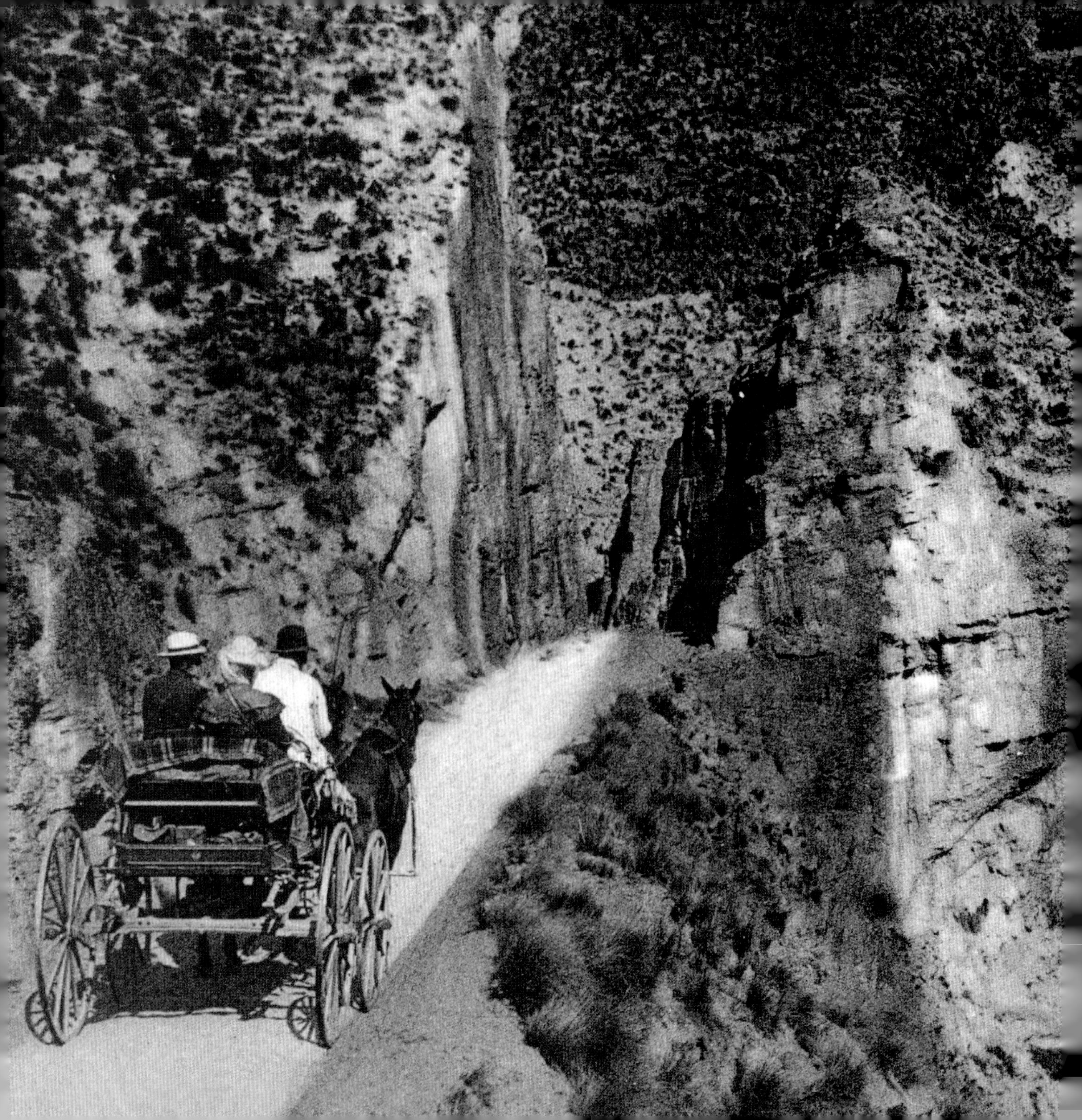

heritage

The historic atmosphere of Skippers is unique and there has long been an awareness that the area's heritage needs to be preserved.

The restoration and refurbishment of the original Skippers School and the old Mount Aurum homestead by the Department of Conservation have been major projects. The opening of the restored school was a nostalgic event for the hundreds of people who turned out, in full period costume and vintage vehicles, to commemorate the occasion in 1992.

Private enterprise has also moved to retain and enhance the history of the area and Winky's Museum, developed by the Hohneck family with its long-time connections with Skippers, tells the Canyon's story well.

Relics of sluicing operations, stamping batteries and a photographic history of the area reflect the beginnings of this remote part of New Zealand.

Remnants of the Bullendale mine that housed the first hydro-electric power plant in New Zealand are also evident in Skippers. An original pipeline, built in 1864 to carry water across the Shotover Canyon to the gold diggings, has been restored and provides a 102 metre (334 feet) high walkway across the river.

The Shotover River has continued over the years to produce gold for modern-day commercial mining ventures. Today several claims are still being worked in the Skippers area.

Left: Hell's Gate Skippers Road c.1910   Right: Welcome Home Inn c.1910

adventure

Skippers and the Shotover River are the focus for innovative adventure activities. While there is no longer bungy jumping from the historic Skippers suspension bridge or the restored Skippers pipeline other extreme activities like the 109 metre (357 feet) Shotover Canyon rope swing have taken its place.

There are numerous "combo" trips in the area combining helicopter flights, jet boating, swings, mountain biking and rafting inspired by the demand for adrenalin activities.

Jet boating and whitewater rafting are synonymous with the Shotover River.

The Shotover Jet, launched in the 1960s, was one of Queenstown's earliest commercial ventures and has an international reputation. It has exclusive rights to the narrow Shotover Canyons and while there have been challenges the local authority has ruled for safety reasons it is a one-operator section of river.

Whitewater rafting exploded on the scene as the adventure sport of the 1980s and enhanced the Shotover River's reputation even further. The river's wild rapids in the rugged scenic valley were a logical target for tourist entrepreneurs.

As with any adventure sport safety is a priority and the once self-regulating industry is now subject to tight controls. Professional river guide training programmes are in place and rafting companies have to measure up on all safety issues. Flouting the rules is viewed seriously by local and national authorities.

The grand finale for the Shotover rafting trips is the Oxenbridge Tunnel. Rafts shoot through a narrow gap to hit a final four metre (13 feet) drop on to the Cascade Rapid. The tunnel is a 170 metre (558 feet) long man-made chute formed when prospectors Ned and Ben Oxenbridge diverted the river to mine the bed. While it cost £10,000 to create the tunnel they only recovered £600 of gold but their efforts left a great bequest for today's thrillseekers.

Left: Shotover Jet   Right: Rafting on Shotover River

43

wakatipu countryside

Farming was once the lifeblood of the Wakatipu Basin but there are few traditional economic farming units left in the district.

The rural landscape of the 21st century differs dramatically from the early pioneering days. Original farms have been split up to provide lifestyle blocks or smaller horticultural and grapegrowing units.

There is intense focus on the countryside and the preservation of the landscape. Far reaching rural planning controls are constantly being reviewed as the community comes to grips with the pressure of growth.

Rural landowners, developers and local authority planners have tended to clash over future direction. While most want to see the rural area protected there's a range of views on how it should be achieved.

Contentious planning legislation has led to strict rules imposed by the Environment Court to protect the landscape and the visual environment for future generations.

Speargrass Flat, Dalefield and Lower Shotover located between Queenstown and Arrowtown epitomise the Wakatipu countryside. The early farmers left a legacy of magnificent trees and remarkable buildings for future residents. Many of those buildings have been restored and will live on.

The original Miller's Cottage beside Mill Creek on Speargrass Flat Road has outlived the Wakatipu Flour Mill which operated until 1902. Once there was a three-storey wooden mill with space for 30,000 bushels of wheat. The remains of the stone stables are all that is left of this thriving business.

A spectacular avenue of poplar trees frames a set of wrought iron gates marking the entrance to the former Thurlby Estate at Speargrass Flat. Thurlby was the home of German-born entrepreneur Bendix Hallenstein, who set up a magnificent country residence in the late 1860s in keeping with his position, establishing a farming property which set new standards for the Wakatipu.

Ballooning in the Wakatipu

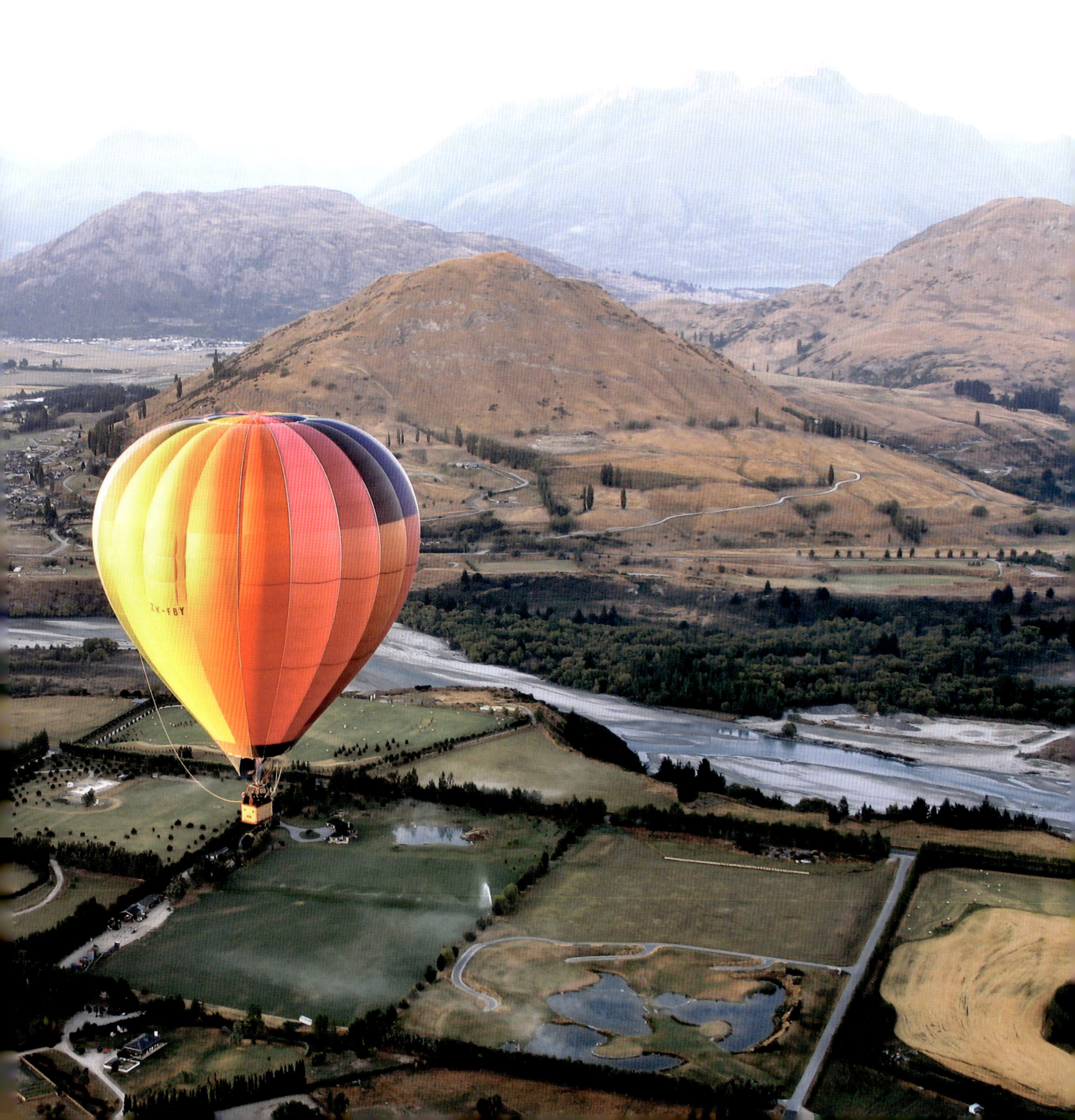
ZK-FBY

Unfortunately many early buildings were not built to last. Thurlby was one which fell into disrepair and has crumbled to ruin since its abandonment in 1946.

The Thurlby outbuildings have fared slightly better. A stable, cattleshed and various outhouses are fine examples of early stone work. Modern day stonemasons have copied the technique and stone walls have been authentically recreated throughout the district.

Hallenstein had a passion for trees. Lebanon Cedars, Mediterranean Cypress, American Sequoia Gigantia, Wellingtonia, English Oaks and other exotics make an impressive line-up today. Two full-time gardeners once worked at Thurlby turning the grounds into an attraction for local people who enjoyed Hallenstein's frequent garden parties.

The grand days of Thurlby may be gone but the inspiration lives on.

The rural charm has attracted artists and craftspeople to live and work in the Wakatipu countryside. Woodworkers, stone and jewellery artists, painters and quiltmakers hang their signs on back country roads. Galleries are dotted throughout the area and an arts trail showcases the homes and studios of some of New Zealand's finest artists.

People who choose to live in the Wakatipu's rural area fiercely guard what they have. Proposed subdivisions are closely monitored and there is a strong desire to avoid overdevelopment of the countryside. However while some rural lifestyle developments have drawn criticism, sensitive projects are supported.

Left: Thurlby Homestead ruins   Right: Thurlby Homestead c.1920

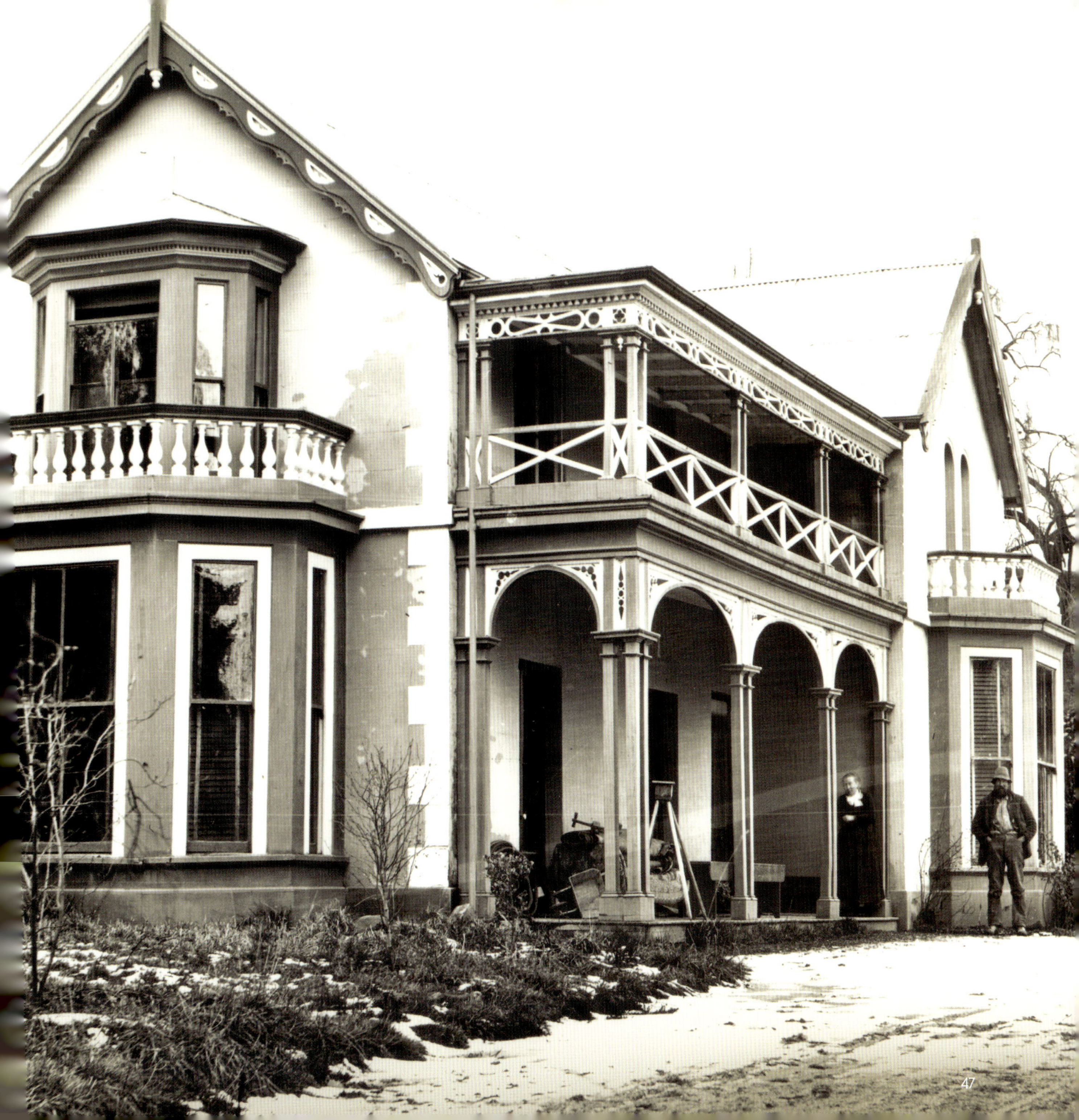

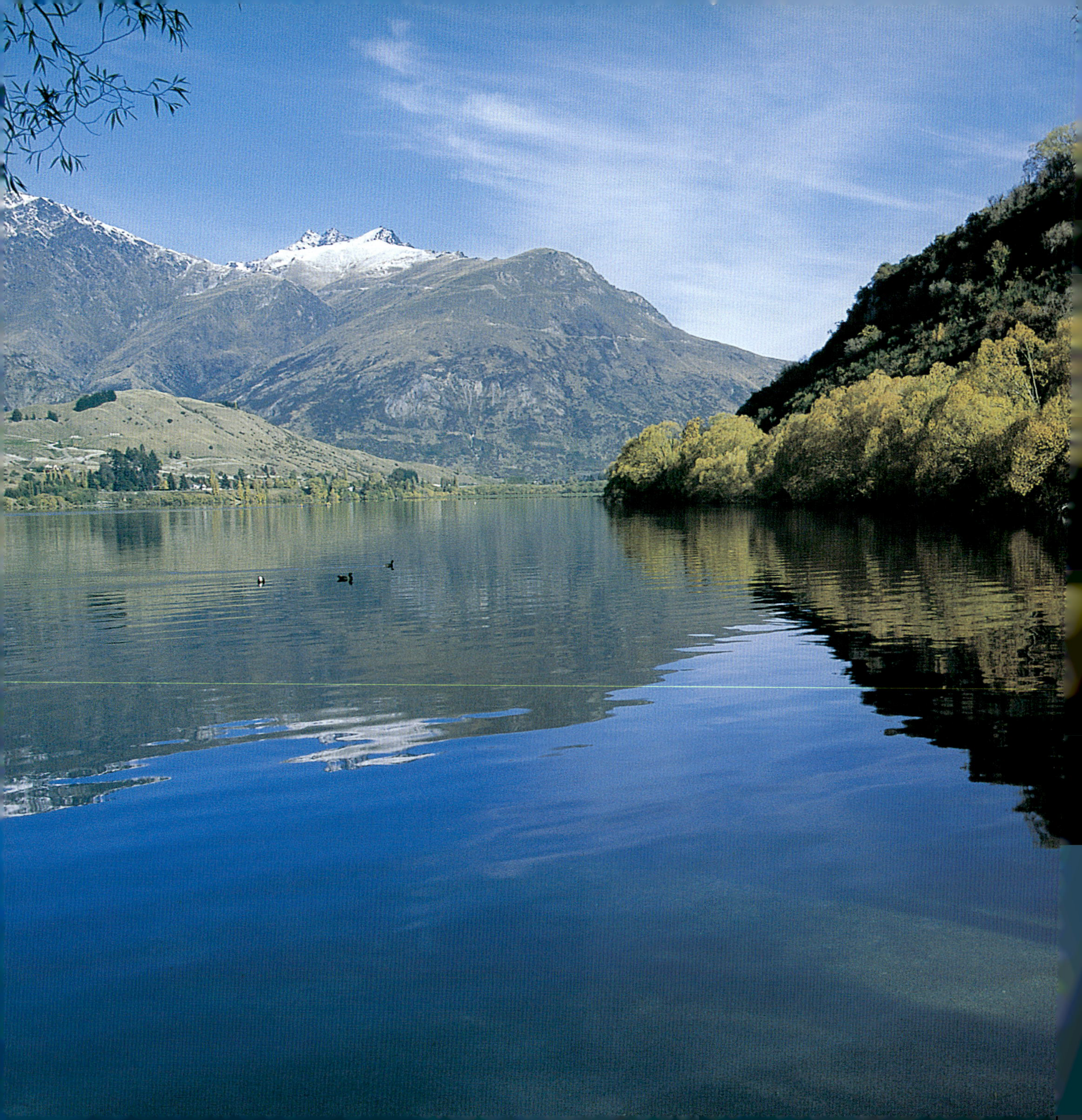

lake hayes

Maori called it Mirror Waters - a fitting description. For mirror-like reflections, deluxe sunsets and unqualified scenic beauty Lake Hayes is out on its own.

But it is more than just a stunning setting.

Lake Hayes, about four kilometres (2.5 miles) long and 30 metres (100 feet) deep, is ranked as the most popular recreational area of its kind in the Wakatipu. It's a great fishing, swimming and picnic spot. Sportspeople, holidaymakers and photographers love it. County shows, multisports events, rowing regattas and scout jamborees all share the Lake Hayes showgrounds venue.

Once just a holiday place Lake Hayes now has a more permanent residential base and lakefront properties, which have high price tags, are sought after.

The Amisfield Wine Company has taken advantage of the backdrop to create an award-winning restaurant and cellar door in a distinctive building overlooking the lake.

Early Wakatipu explorer Donald Hay was the first to discover the lake and by rights it should still be Hay's Lake. But at some stage the name changed to Lake Hayes after the American scoundrel Bully Hayes, an infamous Arrowtown hotel proprietor during the goldrush.

Lake Hayes

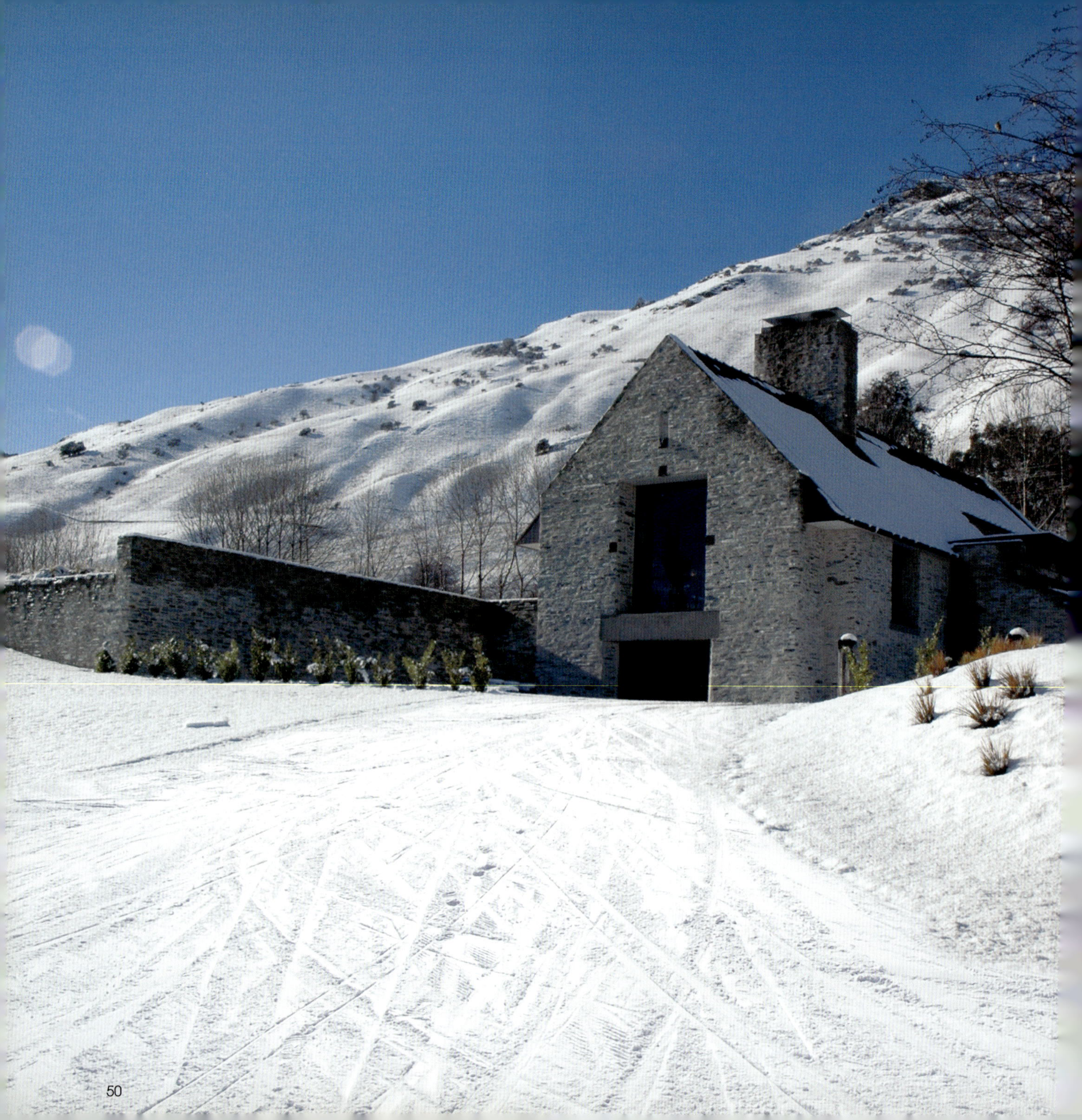

In the 1870s brown trout were introduced to Lake Hayes. This fish did well and so did the poachers. To overcome the poaching problem the White family was given sole rights to net the lake and they ran a commercial fishing operation for many years. The fish smokehouse ruins remain nearby as does the cottage of George White and his family.

White's barn has been converted into a residence with the addition of dormer windows, pergolas and roof shingles. The unusual stone slab wall around the home was originally built as a yard for White's sheep.

Today anglers on the lake comply with a set of rules limiting power boats to eight kilometres an hour (5mph). Trolling must be without a motor and the fishing season is open all year.

A eutrophication problem, which affects the quality of the Lake Hayes water sometimes causing algal bloom during the summer, has been the subject of research over several years and a management strategy has been introduced to control it.

The lake has wildlife refuge status especially for native and introduced birds. Ducks take full advantage of it hiding out in large numbers during the shooting season. The endangered southern crested grebe, shags, hawks and pukekos are regular residents. Less frequent visitors include the kingfisher, white heron and black swan.

A walkway which follows around the shores of Lake Hayes is one of the key Queenstown Trails Trust projects in the district, opening up the previously inaccessible western side of the lake for recreational use by both walkers and mountain bikers. The Trust's strategy is to create an integrated network of walking trails throughout the Wakatipu.

Left: Amisfield Winery Right: Picnicking at Butel Pond c.1899

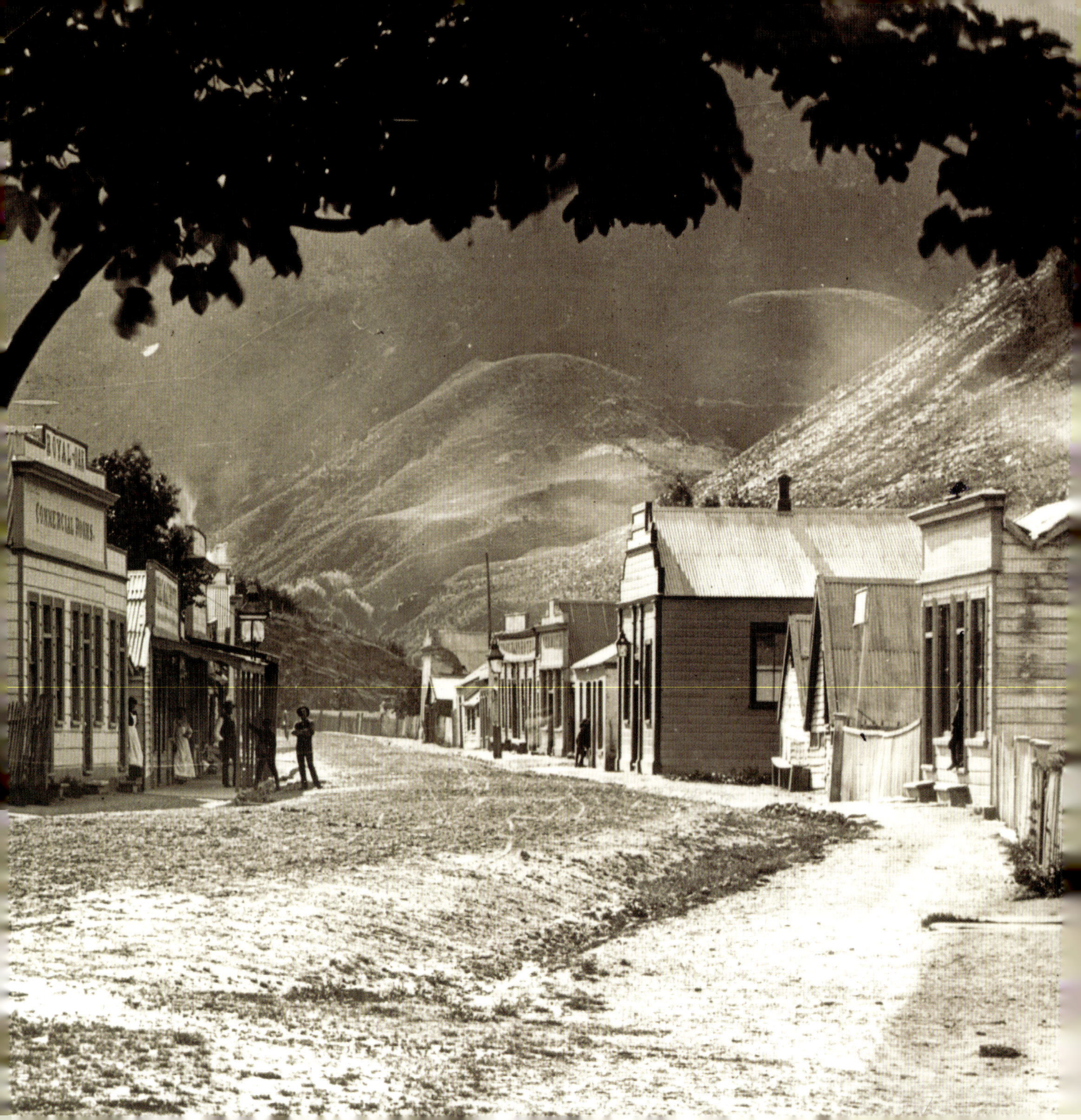
COMMERCIAL ROOMS

arrowtown

Arrowtown is a working museum town and its 19th century character turns back the pages.

Some say it's quaint and others say it's too commercial but whatever Arrowtown has a special charm. The combination of its strong identity, fierce independence and close-knit community is the town's trademark.

Arrowtown was "born of gold." Just a stones's throw from the town the Arrow River washed up enormous amounts of gold. It was easy to get at, there was lots of it and in 1862 miners found it. There were conflicting claims about who was "first" but the distinction apparently went to one William Fox.

Rightly or wrongly Fox made the rules as the unofficial commissioner and Arrowtown was first known as "Fox's Rush" or just "Fox's." The miners soon realised that Fox's was built too close to the goldfields. The chances of nuggets being trapped under the streets were high. But nothing ever came of suggestions to resurvey the town and Arrowtown still stands on the site of the original mining village.

Once the cry of "gold" went out there was a stampede to Arrowtown. Within six months there were about 1500 people at the diggings and at the peak of the rush several thousand people based themselves in or around Arrowtown.

Businesses flourished and men lit their pipes with banknotes. Buckingham Street, still the main street today, bustled with hotels, dance halls and gambling dens. By the end of 1864 Arrowtown had 20 shops, 10 hotels and several private residences. Calico and sod building materials were replaced by iron, stone and timber.

It was not altogether a peaceful community. There were problems with claim jumpers, fighting, and not enough police. Most serious trouble was stopped by the timely arrival of the pistol-wielding Major H.W.Bracken of the Otago Mounted Police.

Where women were concerned there were never enough and most were married off soon after arriving in town.

As the people kept pouring in Arrowtown became overcrowded. Miners trekked their way up the narrow gorge to fresher fields. Over 25 river crossings and 18 kilometres (12 miles) from Arrowtown the settlement of Macetown sprouted. Much smaller than Arrowtown it nevertheless boasted four hotels, four stores, a school, a post office and a public hall.

Macetown grew, prospered and died within the space of 50 years. After the town's demise, the road soon deteriorated. These days it is a four-wheel drive trip or a day tramp or mountain bike ride. There is a sleepy, tranquil atmosphere at the old town site where conservationists have worked hard to preserve the ruins and mining relics.

The Chinese were a colourful group of immigrants to the goldfields, arriving in large numbers around 1869. They were seen as a threat and treated with suspicion but they kept to themselves, happy to work claims abandoned by the Europeans.

They established their community beside Bush Creek tucked amongst the trees on the flats by the Arrow River. After the Chinese left the village virtually disappeared but was unearthed in an archaeological excavation in 1983. Several huts have been rebuilt and the settlement is considered one of the best researched and preserved sites of its kind in New Zealand.

As the goldrush died down many of the miners turned to farming. The industry was boosted in the 1920s when the Arrow River pipeline brought irrigation to most of the Wakatipu.

Buckingham Street c.1890

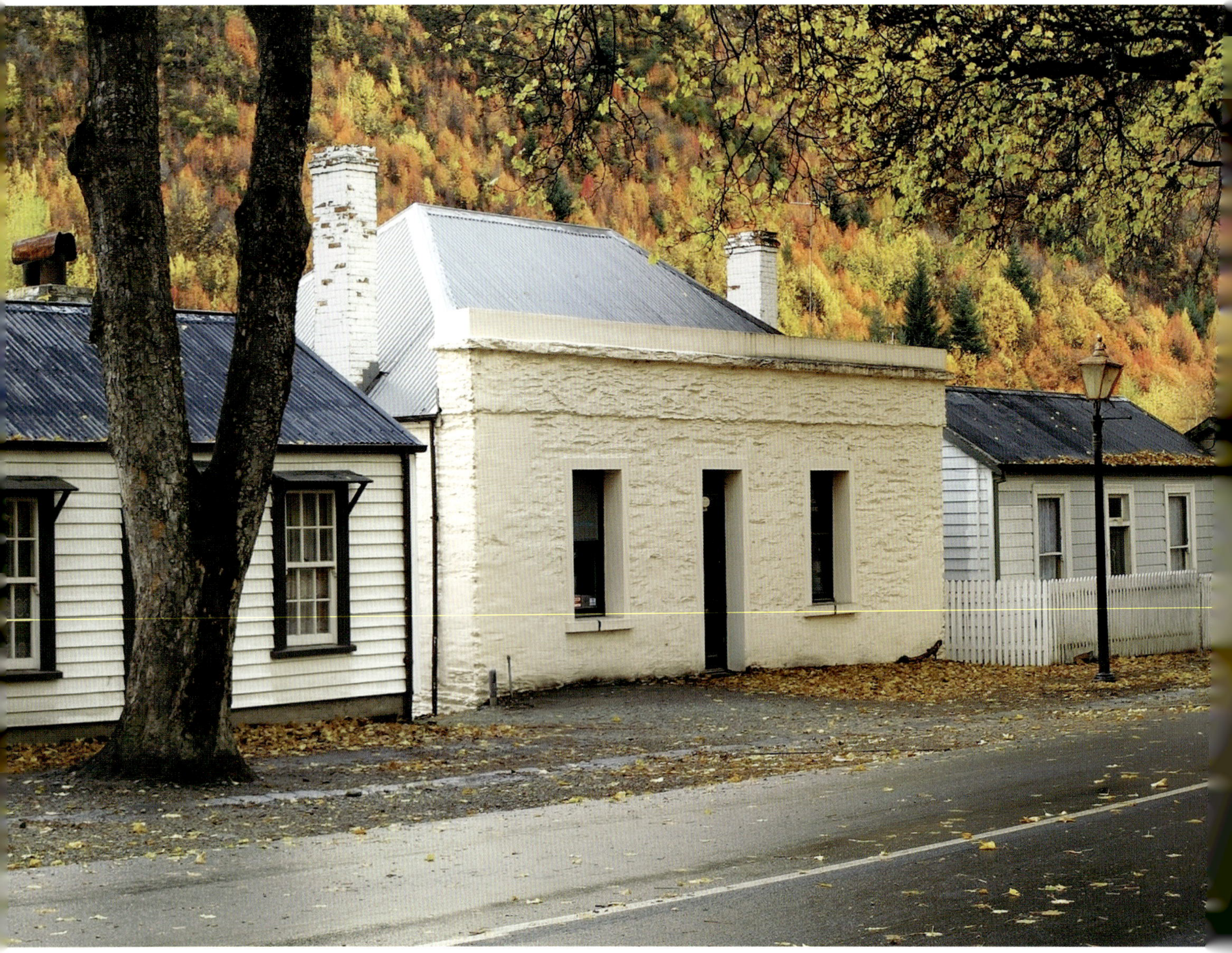

arrowtown today

Modern day Arrowtown retains close links with its colourful past through the preservation of its 19th century architecture.

It is getting harder to pick the old from the new as buildings are skillfully reproduced. The Arrowtown Library received an award for its faithful adherence to the original architectural style, while the Ballarat Shopping Arcade sits well on the site of its predecessor, the Ballarat Hotel. The renowned Royal Oak Hotel has been replaced by a sensitive commercial development.

The replicas are in harmony with the spirit of the town and a strict building code ensures the historic theme is maintained.

Arrowtown people are determined to protect their town. Fears that the 19th century post office would be sold to private developers spurred action by the Lakes District Museum. A petition demanded the building be retained and a deal was struck between New Zealand Post and the Museum. An heritage order has been imposed on both the post office and the adjacent Postmaster's House, providing permanent protection.

The demolition of several original miners' cottages by an overseas property developer was prevented when the Queenstown Lakes District Council, responding to community concerns, purchased the precinct in 2007 and established a community trust to oversee their restoration.

The Lakes District Museum is one of the area's greatest assets. Housed in the former Bank of New Zealand it has been extended over the years and its displays and exhibits do justice to the district's rich past.

Arrowtown Miners' Cottages

Thanks to the foresight of early civic-minded Arrowtown residents English trees line the streets. The elegant deciduous trees - sycamore, poplar, oak and elm - cloak the town with colour during autumn. Arrowtown people celebrate the changing season with a festival for one action-packed week in April.

Fuelled by strong community bonds the festival is always an outstanding success. These same bonds were reflected in Arrowtown's united attempt to fight for its independence during the 1980s. But in spite of its stand Arrowtown was amalgamated with the Queenstown Lakes District bringing to a close 110 years of self-government.

While Arrowtown has always had a small town village atmosphere, the new century has inspired a fresh image. A vibrant café, wine bar, restaurant and shopping scene has developed matching the sophistication of Queenstown.

Arrowtown's population has reached 3000 where it is likely to remain capped due to planning constraints on the expansion of the town boundaries and subsequent residential development.

Close to Arrowtown Millbrook Resort has a mix of hotel accommodation and permanent homes clustered around the fairways of its championship golf course designed by legendary New Zealand golfer Sir Bob Charles.

Millbrook was developed on the site of the historic Mill Farm whose links with the Arrowtown area date back to the 1860s. French immigrant John Butel was the first to see the property's potential and the converted and restored millhouse, blacksmith's shop and stables are witness to the thriving wheat farming and flour operation he set up.

Butel planted the avenue of oaks and elms which form the gateway to the resort. The historic trees have a set a precedent for large scale planting at Millbrook providing a similar inheritance for future generations.

The nearby Hills golf course is privately owned by jewellery entrepreneur Michael Hill. It gained international recognition by hosting the prestigious New Zealand Golf Open and showcasing the region to millions of people worldwide.

Left: The Hills Golf Course Right: Arrowtown Festival Miners' Band

57

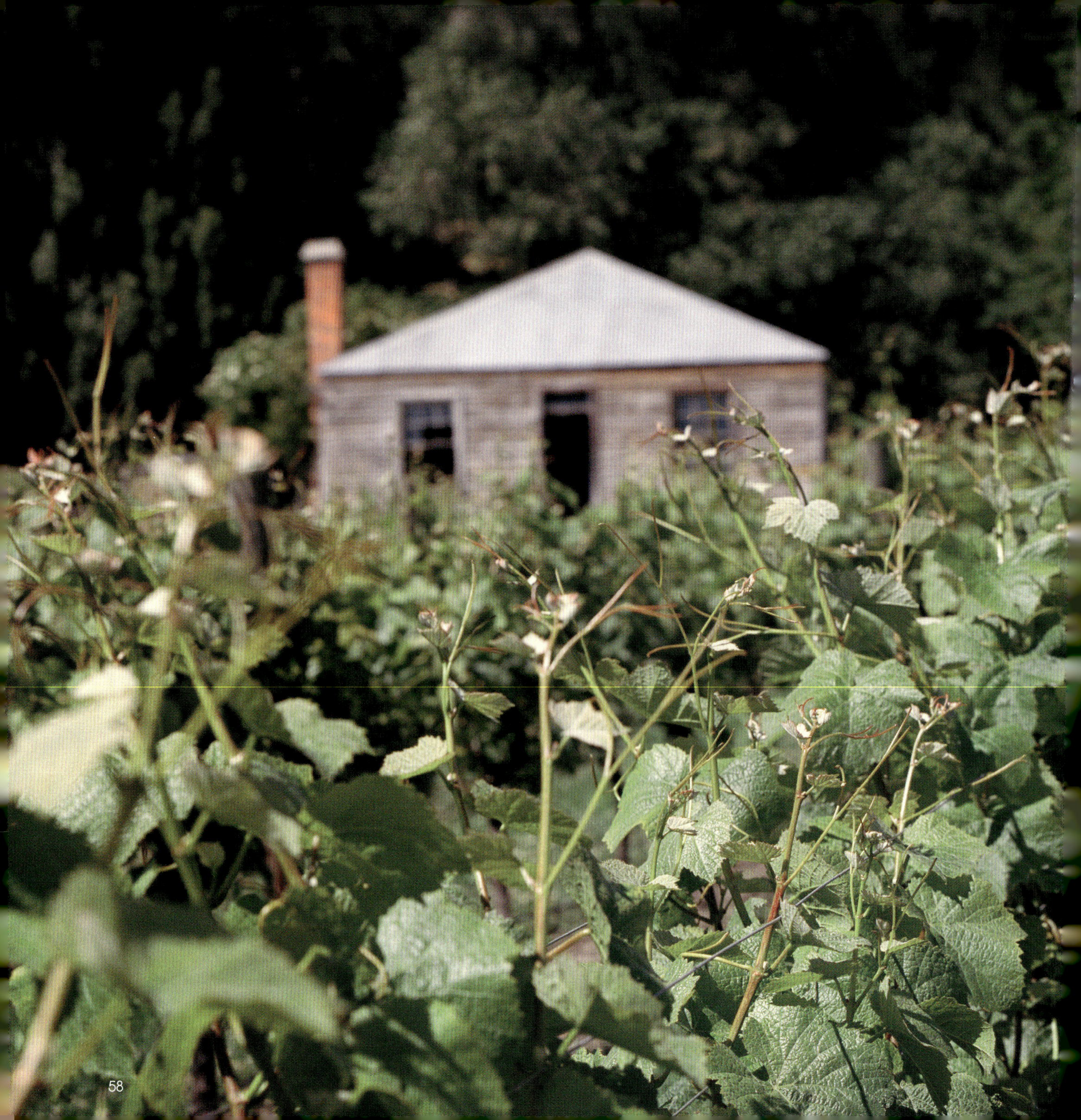

gibbston

The development of the wine industry in Central Otago has had more impact than any other in the last decade.

Widespread grape planting began in the mid-1980s and the region's many vineyards now produce award winning wines, which are exported around the world.

While pockets of the Wakatipu have proved suitable for grapegrowing Gibbston has been the success story.

Close to Arrowtown Gibbston is a geographically unique sub-region of Central Otago, surrounded by mountains and clearly defined boundaries. It is the heart of the local wine industry and its boutique wineries have a national and international profile.

Gibbston Valley and Chard Farm vineyards were the groundbreakers and their early achievements inspired others. Today well known labels including Peregrine, Mount Edward, Mt Rosa, Van Asch, Waitiri Creek, Two Paddocks and Valli Wines are also produced in the valley.

The Central Otago region has a long tradition of viticulture. A hundred years of grapegrowing in Central Otago was celebrated in 1995 commemorating French immigrant Jean Desire Feraud, who pioneered the industry south of Gibbston at Clyde. His Monte Christo wines won early recognition in Australian wine competitions.

Left: Two Paddocks Vineyard
Right: Chard Farm overlooking the Kawarau River

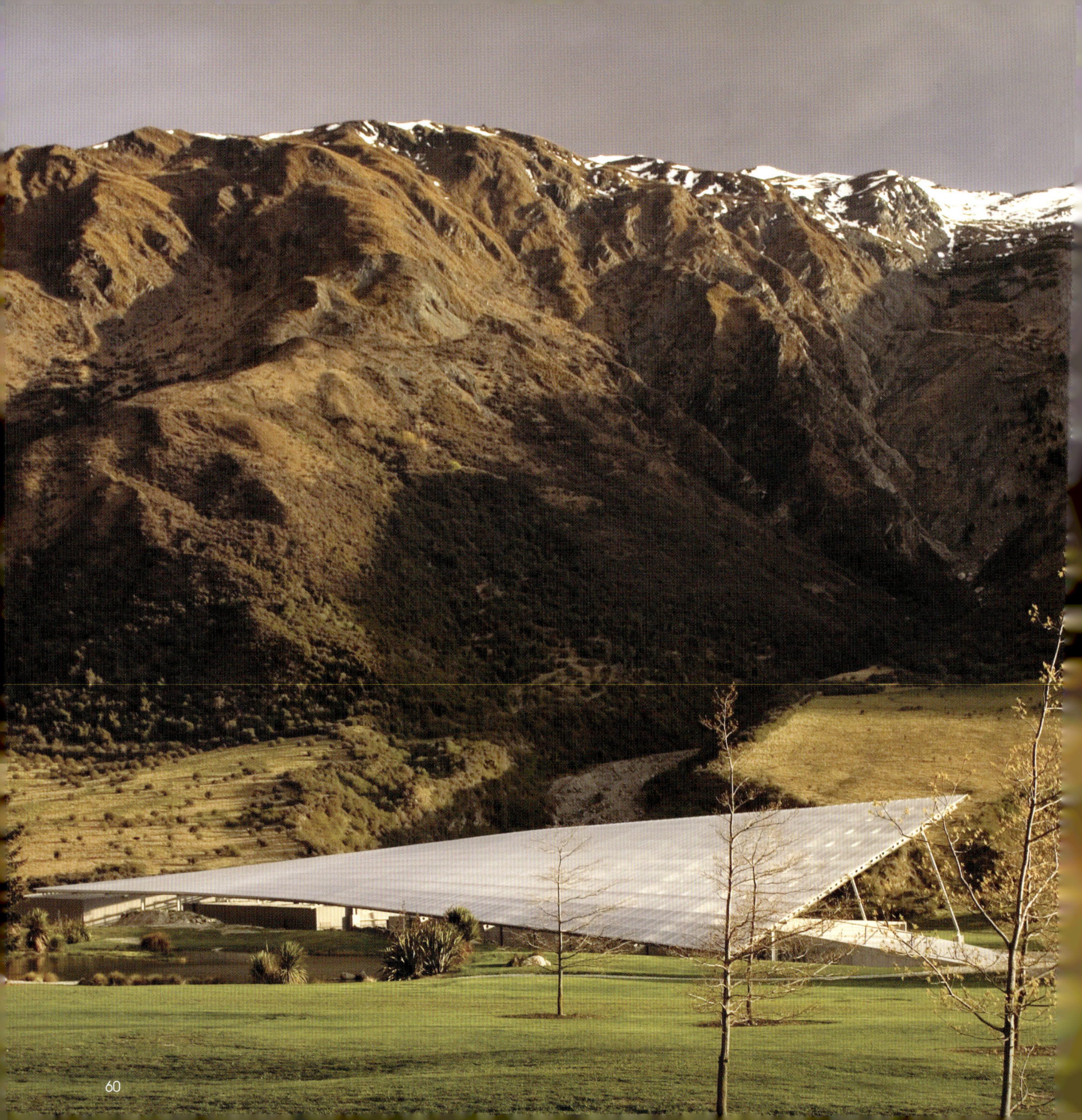

After Feraud left the region there was no commercial winemaking until the 1980s. Sceptics thought the new wine pioneers were taking a huge gamble. "Too cold, too high and too far south" was the catchcry.

But they were proved wrong. The region is on the 45th parallel and is often compared with Burgundy in France. On the same latitude as Bordeaux the area's continental-type climate is ideal. Winemakers have shown that even in a poor season grapes will ripen, although frost damage can be a problem. While the whites do well the area is renowned for its Pinot Noir and a Pinot Noir celebration draws wine growers and critics from all over the world.

Central Otago wineries are billed as the southernmost vineyards in the world and are very much part of the tourist trail. Many have restaurants and tasting facilities and the Gibbston Valley Winery's underground wine caves are a significant attraction. A harvest festival is held in Gibbston every year to celebrate the annual grape harvest.

The spectacular Gibbston River Trail which accesses wineries was opened at the end of 2010 spearheaded by the active Gibbston Community Association.

Gibbston was originally a farming settlement. Surrounded by many large rural properties it had its own school and even a hotel. They are long gone but the historic Kawarau suspension bridge built in 1880 still remains.

No longer used for traffic the bridge has a new lease of life as a world famous bungy jumping site. Bungy entrepreneur AJ Hackett launched his New Zealand bungy jumping venture on the 43 metre (141 feet) Kawarau Bridge in 1988. The Department of Conservation allowed the concession in exchange for the restoration of the near-derelict bridge.

Bungy jumping became so popular that just over a year after it started the bridge underwent a $100,000 facelift extending its life for another 100 years.

Gibbston may be just a small mark on the map but its future is bright, reinforced by the commitment of the new entrepreneurs and a dedicated community.

Left: Peregrine Winery
Right: Bungy Jumping at Kawarau Suspension Bridge

mountains

Winter transforms Queenstown into a playground for skiers and snowboarders from around the world.

Until the 1940s Queenstown was purely a summer resort but skiing changed that. Two major ski areas, Coronet Peak and The Remakables, with quite different but complementary terrain, are so close to Queenstown they are literally in the town's backyard.

Skifield development was influenced in 1947 by the Mount Cook Group which had already pioneered road services and airlines into the region.

To talk of the early Mount Cook Company is really to talk of the Wigley family. They were an enterprising family headed by Rodolph Wigley who drove the first car across the gruelling Crown Range route from Wanaka to Queenstown in 1924. This was the forerunner to the company's coach service expanding into a national network.

The company identified commercial skiing opportunities in Queenstown early on and the first hut was installed on Coronet Peak in 1940. Skiing the hard way - without lifts - was launched and it was a favourite pastime for locals to trek up the mountain and ski down.

Seven years later the first rope tow was installed and a Norwegian ski instructor hired. Coronet Peak with its diverse range of slopes was the perfect mountain and the sport never looked back.

The first Pomalgaski chairlift was in place by 1964 and expansion over the years has seen the installation of triple, quad and six-seater chairlifts, T-Bars, learner lifts and terrain parks.

Rodolph Wigley passed on to his son Harry, later to become Sir Henry, the fire for adventure and achievement. It was Sir Henry who had the vision for a ski area in the Remarkables Mountains. As a pilot he had flown over the range many times and seen the potential.

The Mount Cook Group was hard to convince but by the mid 1970s he had persuaded the company to take the project seriously.

The Remarkables planning process was controversial. There was strong opposition from people claiming it was a sacrilege to scar the mountainside with a road and turn the wilderness area into a commercial venture. It took years to overcome the planning hurdles but in the early 1980s the company finally won approval. Sir Henry Wigley had been the driving force but sadly did not live to see his dream realised.

Building the high-altitude road was a major feat. It took two years and was completed in 1985. Soon there were two quad chairlifts, a double chair and beginners' tows at the new ski area.

There is an international awareness of Queenstown as a ski destination. The concept of combining skiing with other outdoor adventure and recreational activities has wide appeal and Queenstown is the only Australasian ski area included in the prestigious Leading Mountain Resorts of the World partnership, along with five other destinations in Europe, South America and the United States.

Coronet Peak and the Southern Alps

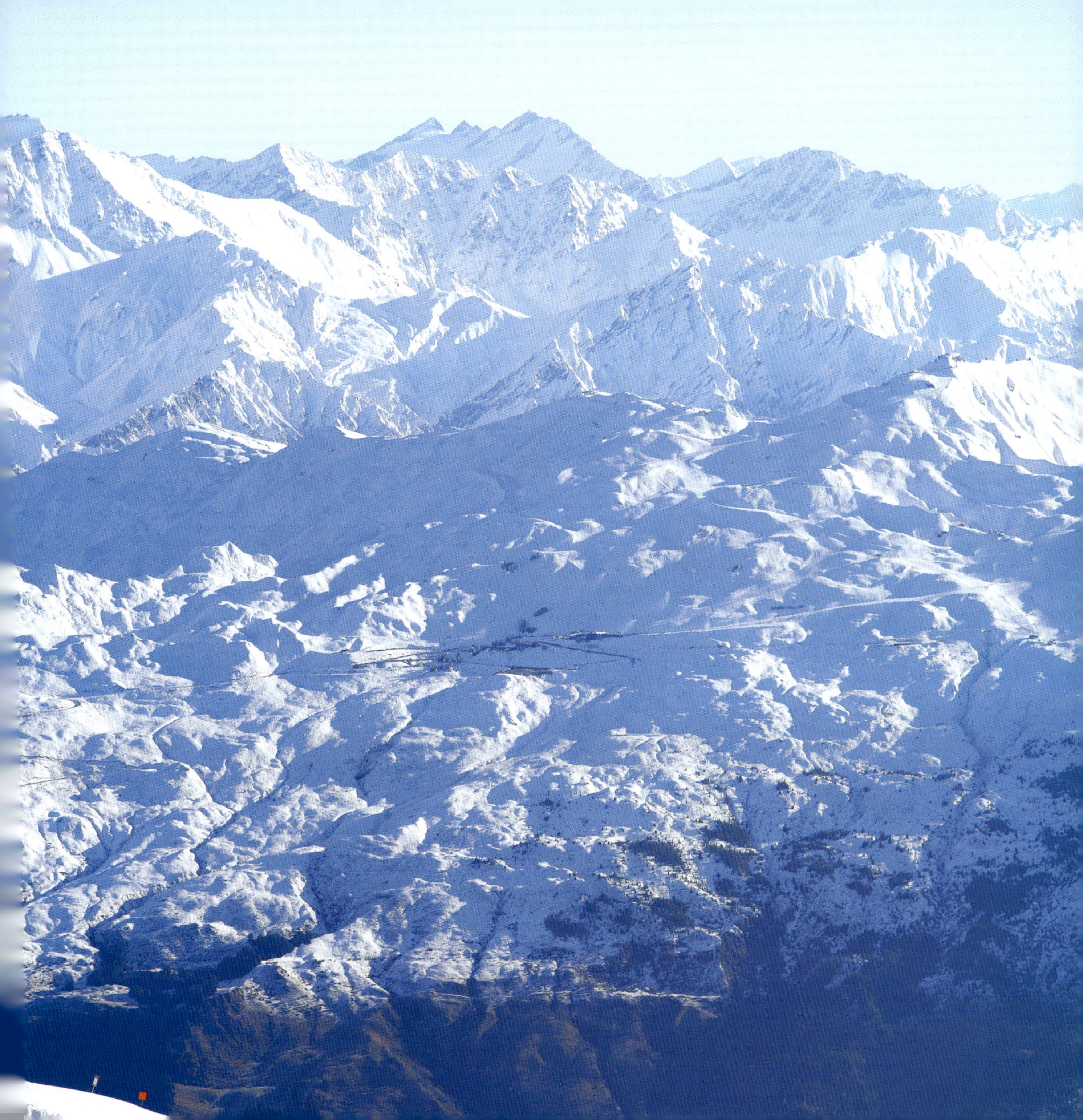

coronet peak

Diehard Coronet Peak fans won't ski or ride anywhere else. The mountain is addictive and has variety and challenge.

Coronet Peak has 280 hectares (690 acres) of versatile slopes taking in steep faces, tough bumps and gentle rolling runs. Each slope has its own identity and every season there's a new option on the trails.

Extensive snowmaking means the snow starts to fall as soon as the temperature drops. Machine-made snow ensures a consistently early start to the season and the snow guns work throughout the winter boosting natural snowcover.

Winter Festival Dog Derby

The original double and triple chairlifts have made way for high-speed quad and six-seater lifts accessing a huge variety of terrain. Learners' facilities include an express chairlift and beginners' carpet lifts while a t-bar operates in Rock Gully.

The Peak has an international team of skiing and snowboarding instructors who add a cosmopolitan flavour to mountain activities. Overseas ski racing teams seeking off-season training grounds, particularly in their build-up to World Cup events and the Winter Olympics, target Coronet Peak with its purpose-built race training arena in Rocky Gully.

The Winter Games New Zealand are held every two years in Queenstown and Coronet Peak hosts the alpine events attracting top ranked international athletes.

The mountain always has a festive atmosphere and comes into its own during Queenstown's annual winter festival.

The festival transforms the ski area. Rock music pulsates through the mountain air, ice carvers create masterpieces and serious and not so serious competitions are features of the ten day programme.

Coronet Peak is just as appealing at night. When the sun goes down the lights come on and night skiing continues under blazing floodlights.

the remarkables

The Remarkables picks up where Coronet Peak leaves off.

The higher, northwest facing Remarkables Ski Area was designed to complement the skiing tradition on the other side of the valley. It is more of a family area with a slant to the slopes that suits less advanced skiers. But there is plenty of challenge for experts too.

Set in 220 skiable hectares (550 acres) Shadow Basin, the Sugar Bowl and Alta are the three main ski runs accessed by quad chairlifts. The Alta takes care of beginners and graduates on to the Sugar Bowl's good intermediate country. The Shadow Basin chair gives access to steep chutes dropping down to the glacial Lake Alta. Skyline trails lead to the 1.5 kilometre (1 mile) Homeward Bound slope, New Zealand's longest back-country ski run.

The Remarkables' unique terrain provides endless options. Snowboarders are well catered for with a testing terrain park and freeskiers and extreme skiers love the challenging faces. From an altitude of about 2000 metres (6500 feet) there are stunning views stretching over the entire Wakatipu Basin.

The high standard of base facilities, ski school, slope grooming and international trail signs is carried over from Coronet Peak. Snowmaking at The Remarkables also helps reinforce heavily used trails.

The Remarkables is a popular spring skiing mountain. A spring festival attracts people from all over to compete in zany events such as the water jump and riding rubber rafts on snow.

Ski area development has also opened up the alpine area for trampers and tourists keen to escape into the mountains in summer.

Everyone has their preference and while Coronet Peak and Remarkables Ski Areas each have their own identity they are an ideal combination.

Right: The Remarkables Ski Area
Page over: Freeskiing at the Remarkables

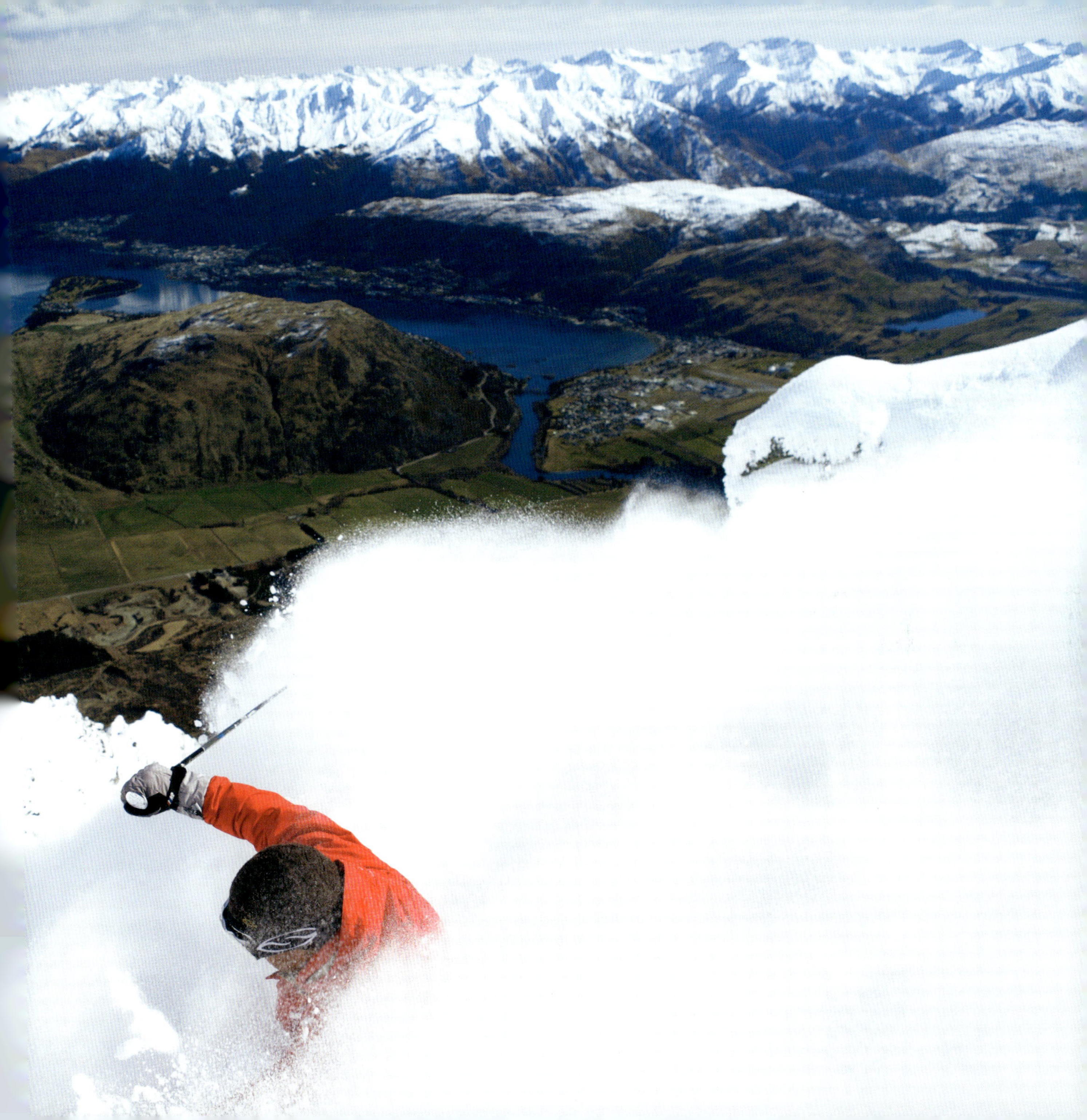

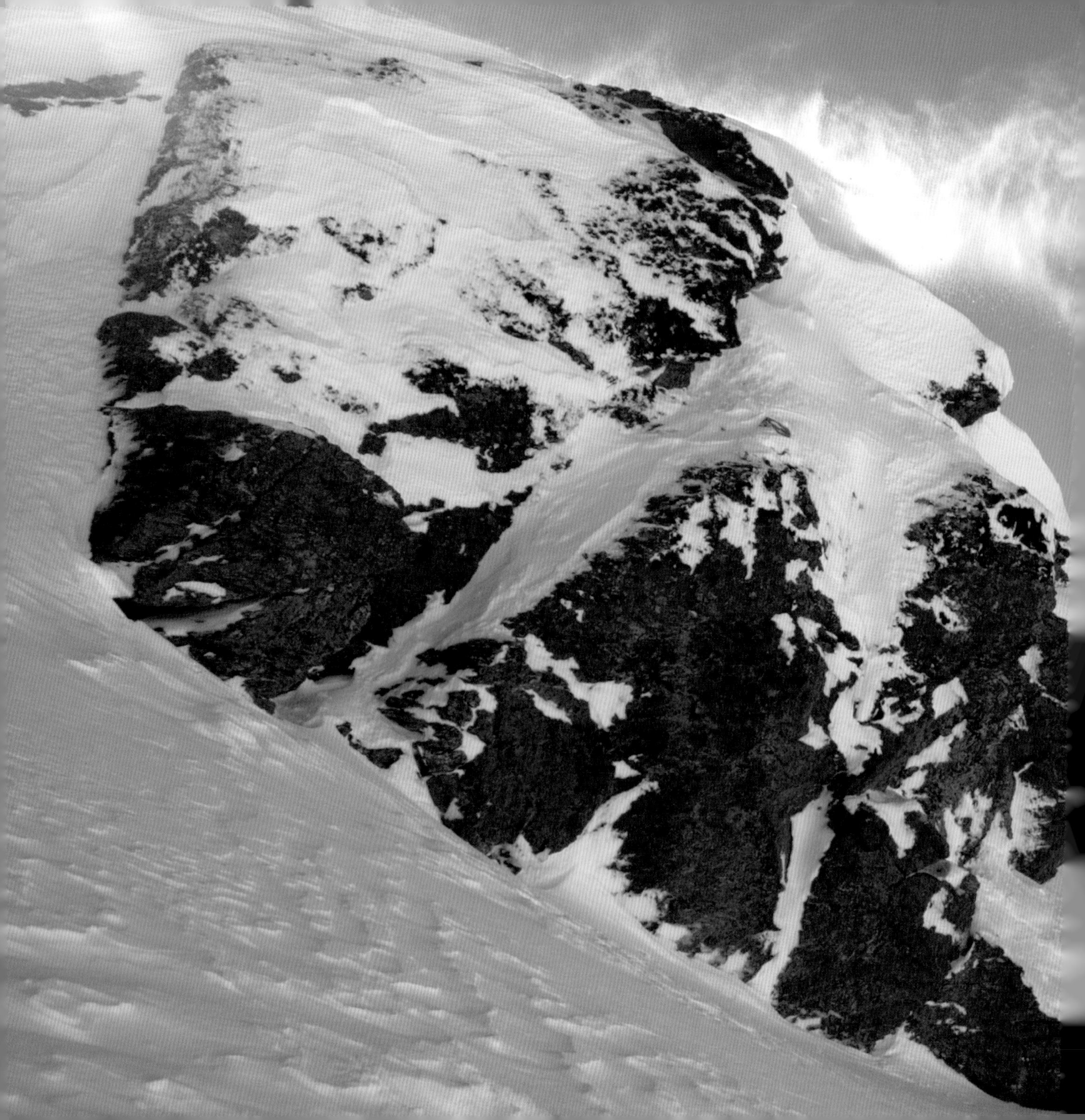

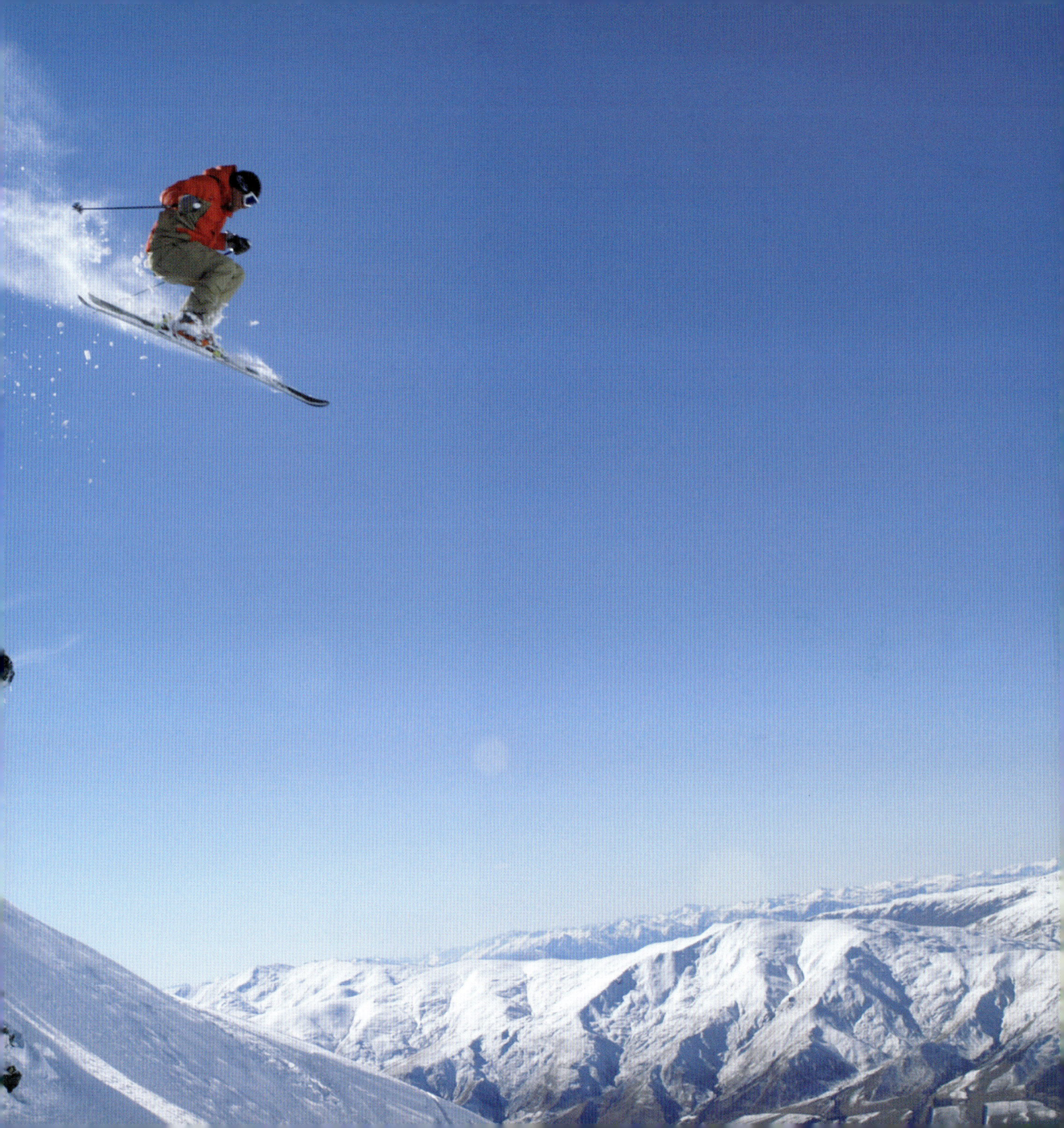

helicopters

Heli-skiing and heli-boarding are compulsory for snow seekers looking for the ultimate in adventure. Untouched powder slopes, miles from anywhere, where the only access is by helicopter.

The sport has opened up new recreation areas in remote mountain areas and cemented the helicopter's role even further in the tourism industry.

The advent of the helicopter brought a new dimension to tourism and its influence has been significant. Scenic flights around the region taking in spectacular mountain peaks operate all year round and there are any number of helicopter combination tourist rides.

It started with the heli-jet in the late 1970s when two enterprising young jet boat operators were faced with a business downturn after floods prevented them operating their Lake Wakatipu-Kawarau River jetboat trip. They based their boat on the river and flew passengers there by helicopter. It was an instant success and the heli-jet was launched.

The "heli-concept" caught on and today there's heli-rafting, heli-walking, heli-biking and even heli-fishing.

Queenstown is a sought after international movie location and helicopters are vital for aerial filming and ferrying crew and gear around. Peter Jackson's *Lord of the Rings* trilogy was filmed in the region and helicopters, fitted with specially developed camera systems, were an integral part of the techniques required to produce the award-winning series.

High country farmers use helicopters as a workhorse to shift men and dogs into the rugged backcountry for their annual musters. For rural firefighting the helicopter is indispensable.

One of its most significant roles is in rescue work. Helicopters are an essential life support machine for rescues in the mountains and the backcountry. Many climbers and trampers owe their lives to pilots who undertake rescue missions in the hills and mountains around Queenstown, often in risky conditions.

Helicopter pilots are the unsung heroes of rescues and their feats often go unrecognised. For most "it is all in a day's work" but without their commitment and courage many people would not survive.

The Lakes District Air Rescue Trust is the core of the air rescue and air ambulance service in the region. The combined efforts of the local helicopter operators have created one of New Zealand's most efficient and effective services.

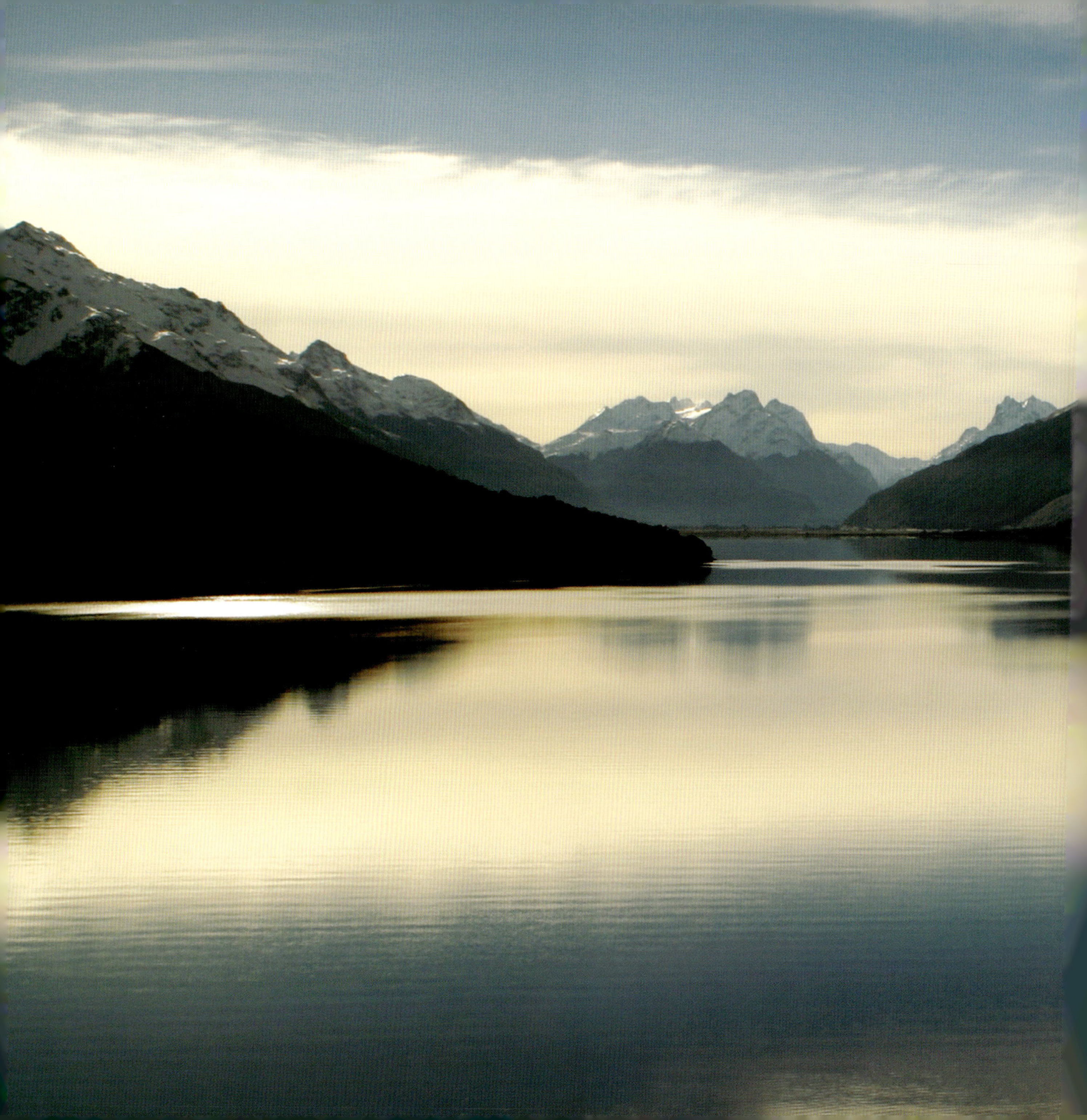

glenorchy

The sign says "Welcome to Paradise." This is Glenorchy - first impressions of the town may not be much but the scenery more than compensates.

Nestled at the head of Lake Wakatipu, at the foot of the Richardson Mountains and looking out to the Humboldt Mountains, Mount Earnslaw and the Rees Valley, this is no ordinary backdrop.

Glenorchy may be small but it has an extensive and rich history.

Goldmining, scheelite mining, sawmilling and farming have supported the community through the years. Tourism also got off to an early start and today thousands of people visit the head of the lake to experience the great outdoors - to tramp, climb, hunt, fish and jet boat.

Glenorchy's first inhabitants were shepherds and goldminers. Gold was mined in pockets all around the area, but with less success than in other fields. The main mining venture was the Invincible Mine in the Rees Valley where a stamp battery was used to crush the gold-bearing quartz. The first crushing in November 1882 yielded 325 ounces of gold. All that remains are parts of the large water wheel which drove the stamp battery and other relics of mining machinery.

The Head of Lake Wakatipu

For a long time Glenorchy's lifeline was scheelite. The ore lacked the dazzle of gold but the cash return was better. The town matured during the two world wars when scheelite was used to make tungsten to produce weapons. With the outbreak of war in Korea in 1950 miners poured back into the hills when scheelite prices rose to previously unheard of levels. Up until 1961 New Zealand produced just over 1000 tons of scheelite and most of it came from Mount Juda just behind the Glenorchy township.

Nowadays prices are low, costs of extraction are high and the numerous claims still staked in the hills lie idle.

The head of Lake Wakatipu has also been an important source of timber and several sawmills operated until the 1950s producing timber for bridge construction for the mines and the farming community. A thriving mill operated at Kinloch, Glenorchy's twin settlement, in the 1800s. This source of timber came to an end after a series of bushfires scarred the beautiful spot.

From the late 1880s farms were settled but the going was tough. Difficult conditions and isolation from the markets have always been an issue for Glenorchy farmers and now only a few farming properties remain.

Rees Valley

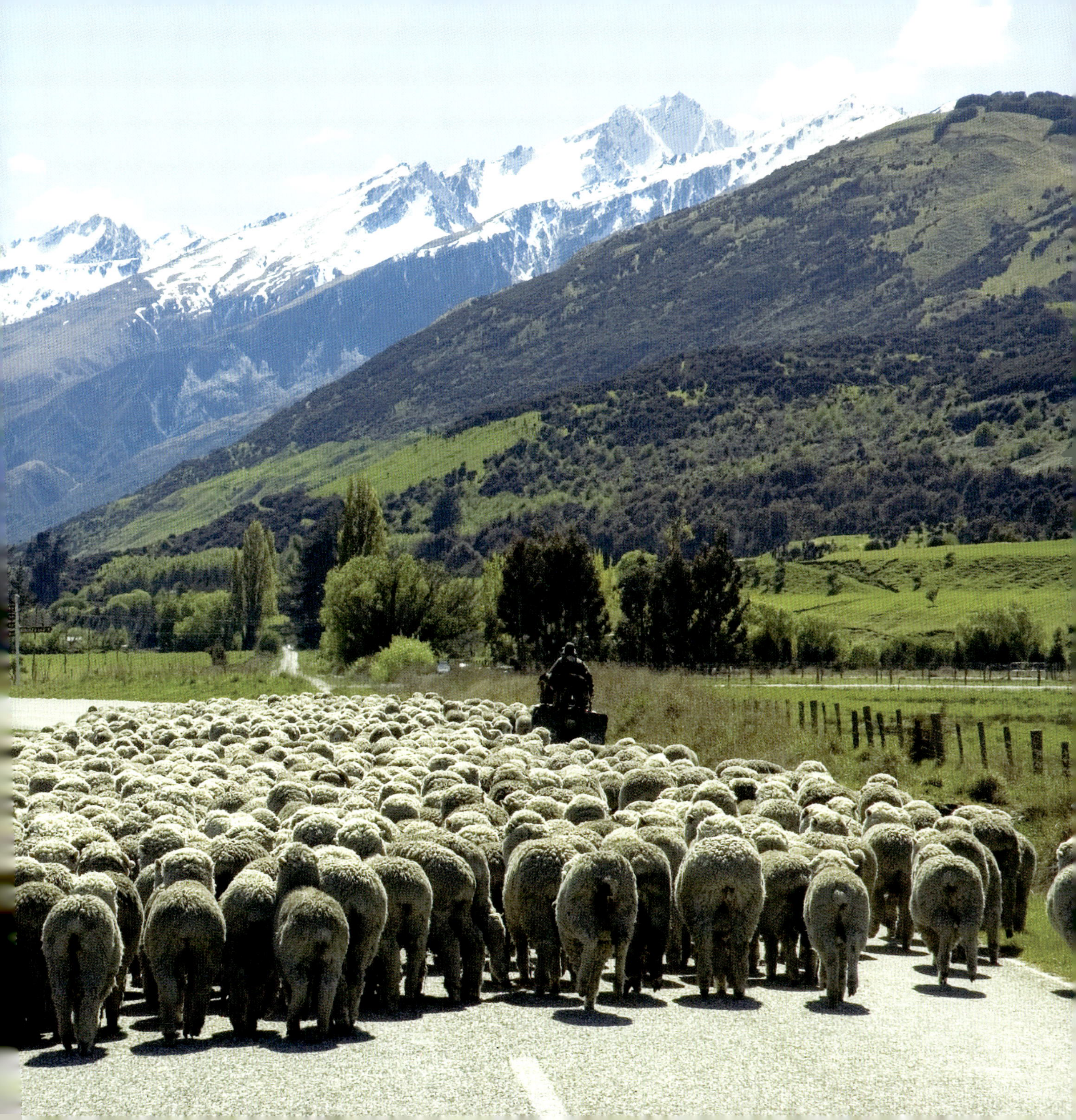

tourism

The early tourist trade at Glenorchy evolved between 1890 and 1930 and focused on steamship services on Lake Wakatipu. Connecting bus tours took in the Routeburn Valley, through lush beech forests and scenic spots such as Diamond Lake, Lovers Leap and Paradise.

The Bryant family ran a high profile tourist business from a base at Kinloch operating bus trips around the area and to the Routeburn Valley. The tours were linked with the TSS Earnslaw's timetable until the steamer was withdrawn from the head of the lake route in 1968. The Bryant's original home is now a guest lodge at Kinloch and the company's bus has been restored and is a distinctive sight again on the Wakatipu roads.

Tourist accommodation and hotels sprang up in the early 1880s. Three hotels were open in Glenorchy by 1885, Kinloch had the Glacier Hotel and Paradise House and the Arcadia guest house were built at Paradise. Today there is a mix of hotel, motel and lodge accommodation including the exclusive luxury retreat Blanket Bay.

Glenorchy has undergone notable change since its road link with Queenstown opened in 1962. The winding, narrow and rough 50 kilometre (31 miles) road had a notorious reputation and its maintenance was costly for Queenstown Lakes district ratepayers.

The breakthrough came in the early 1990s when the Glenorchy road was declared a special purpose route attracting Government funding to seal the highway.

Over the years Glenorchy has had its setbacks and one of the biggest blows was the closing of the town's post office in 1988. The tiny head of the lake school also suffers from fluctuations in pupil numbers which can affect funding and teaching positions.

Setbacks aside though steady growth has taken place. A bridge built across the Dart River in 1974 helped by providing road access to places like Kinloch and the Greenstone and Caples and Routeburn walking tracks.

There has been much talk over the years about a road link between the Greenstone and Milford Sound to provide a unique tourist trip. It has never eventuated but other proposals have surfaced aimed at shortening the trip from Queenstown to Milford Sound.

There was a groundswell of opposition to plans for a monorail through the Greenstone Valley in the early 1990s. Thousands of people all over New Zealand petitioned Parliament to protect the valley. Plans for a multi-million dollar high-speed gondola linking the area to Milford have also been promoted along with a separate proposal to build a tunnel between the Mount Aspiring and Fiordland National Parks shortening the distance between Queenstown and Milford Sound.

The Glenorchy area, particularly Paradise, has attracted intense interest from moviemakers and commercial producers in recent years. The head of the lake was the backdrop for many scenes in the *Lord of the Rings* series, inspiring Middle-Earth tours to the film location sites. The region also features in *The Chronicles of Narnia*.

While Glenorchy is widely recognised as a significant tourist destination the small local community is committed to projects to benefit the town. It is best known for its annual fundraising picnic races when station hacks come from around the district, some even by barge across Lake Wakatipu, to compete. The event attracts huge crowds and is an important source of funds for community groups.

Left: Dart River funyaks   Right: Bryant's Tours c.1950

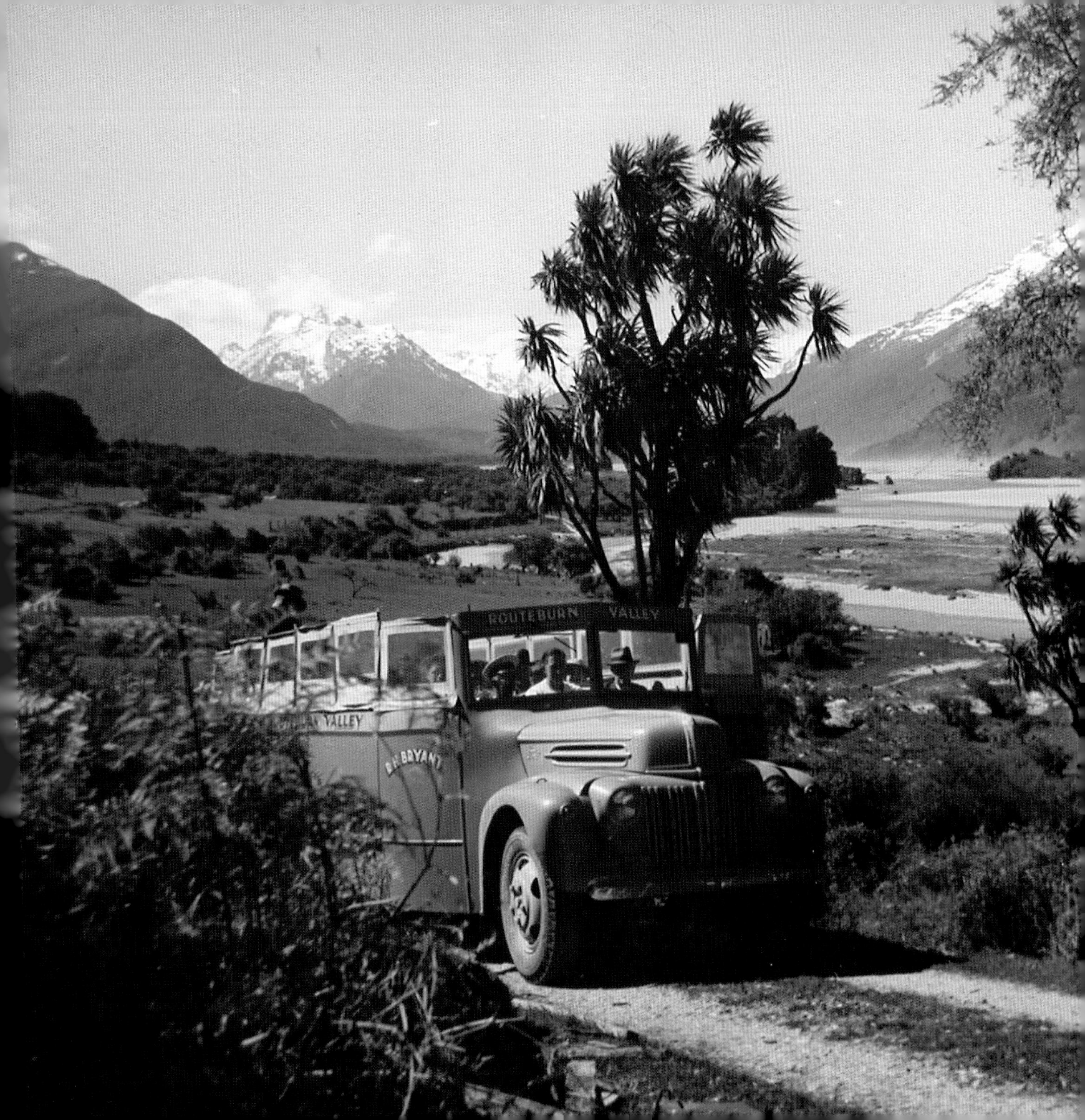
ROUTEBURN VALLEY

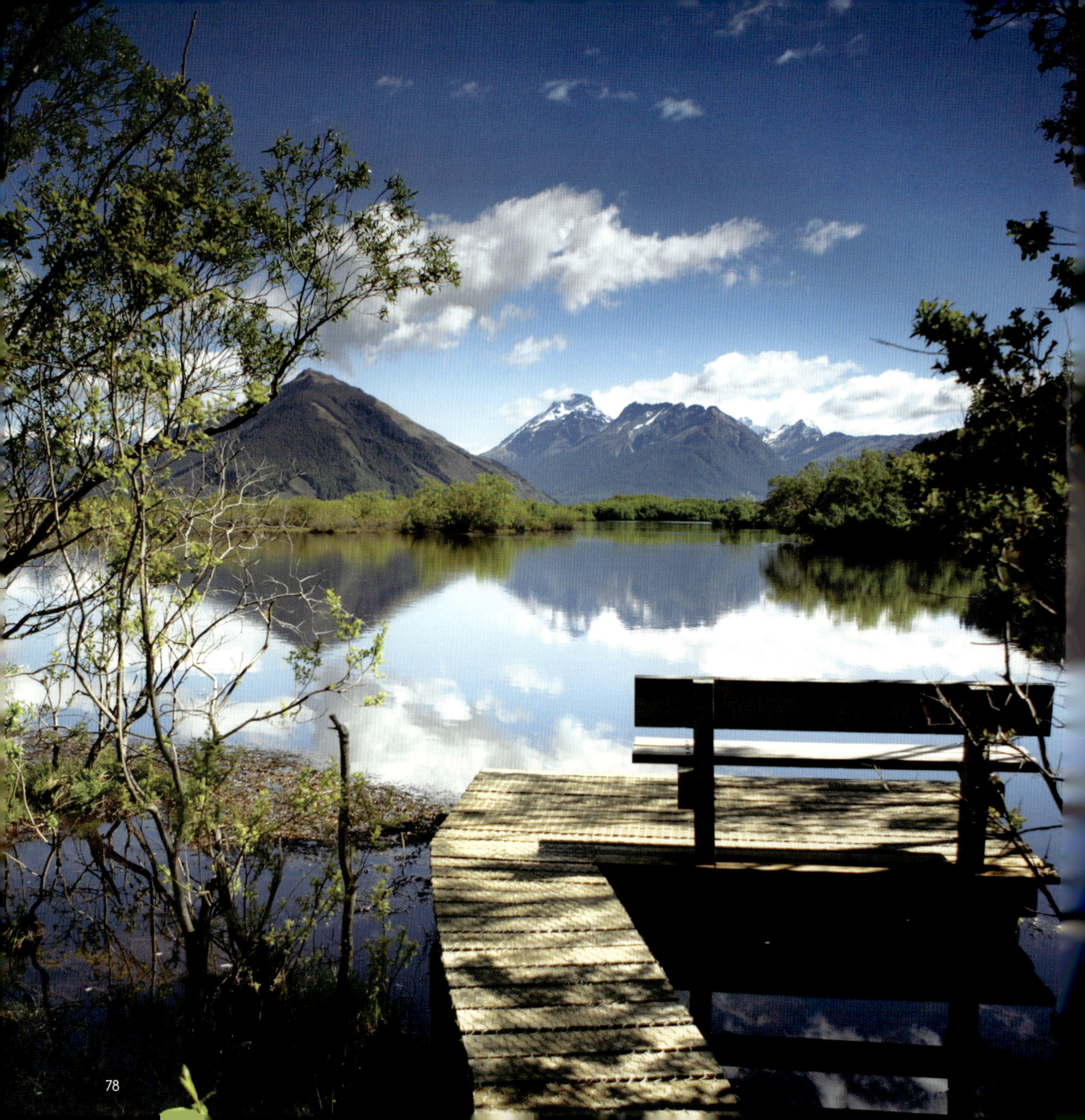

recreation

Glenorchy is the launching pad to Mount Aspiring National Park, home of New Zealand's most famous walking tracks.

The best known is the Routeburn Track which is so popular that there is now a booking system for the Department of Conservation public huts to ensure everyone gets a bed. Many of the walkers are overseas visitors and thousands "do it" every year. Private guided walks, with their own network of lodges on the Routeburn and the Greenstone Valley tracks, are operated by Ultimate Hikes and have an international reputation.

Glenorchy is also the departure point for the Rees and Dart Valley walks and numerous shorter treks around the area. The Dart River is a spectacular setting for jetboating and canoeing in one of the region's most dramatic wilderness areas.

Mountains in the area hold challenges and Mt Earnslaw 2819 metres (9249 feet), the highest in the district next to Mt Aspiring 3027 metres (9928 feet), towers over the Rees and Dart Valleys and Lake Wakatipu's northern arm. Its twin peaks offer a choice of an easier route and a tough technical climb.

Not quite as demanding but equally as exciting is windsurfing. Windsurfers claim Glenorchy is the fastest official sailing spot in the world and there are regular attempts to set new international windsurfing speed records here.

Glenorchy's reputation as a recreational and eco-tourism playground is well established and can only continue to flourish.

Left: Glenorchy Lagoon   Right: Routeburn Track

references

Irene Adamson Queenstown. Bascands Ltd 1985
Marion Borrell Old Buildings of the Lakes District. David Johnston 1973
F.W.G.Miller Golden Days of Lake County. Whitcombe and Tombs Ltd 1962
R.J.Meyer All Aboard. NZ Railway and Locomotive Society Inc. 1980

Florence Preston Out and About in Queenstown. A.H.& A.W.Reed 1976
John Bell Thomson Swiftly Flows the Arrow. John McIndoe Ltd 1985
Harry Wigley Ski Plane Adventure. A.H.& A.W. Reed 1965
King Wakatip G.J. Griffiths. John McIndoe Ltd Dunedin. 1971

contributors

Compact Productions sincerely thanks the following for their photographic contributions:

Aaron McLean (page 58)
AJ Hackett Bungy (page 61)
Hilton Queenstown (page 35)
Hohneck Family (page 39)
Darren Caulton (pages 72-73, 78)
Dart River Safaris (page 76)
Destination Queenstown (pages 54-55)
Hilton Queenstown (page 35)
Jacks Point Queenstown (pages 29, 80)
Kawarau Jet (page 27)
Lakes District Museum (archive photographs - pages 20, 21, 22, 26, 36, 40, 41, 47, 51, 52, 77)

Nomad Safaris (page 38)
NZSki (pages 63, 66-67, 68-69) Miles Holden www.nzski.com
Peregrine Winery (page 60)
Queenstown Rafting (page 43)
Queenstown Winter Festival/Barry Harcourt (pages 11, 64)
Real Journeys (pages 24-25, 30)
Scott Conway Feast Creative (page 50)
Shotover Jet (page 42)
Southern Lakes Heliski (pages 70 - 71)
Skyline Enterprises (page 10)
Sunrise Balloons (pages 44-45)
The Hills/Mark Hill (page 56)
Ultimate Hikes (page 79)